The

WAY OF TRANSFORMATION

This book is designed for those moments where the full-size edition is too bulky. Slip it in your pocket and go!

It is **important to note** that this pocket size edition contains the transcribed lessons only. It does **not include** the foreword, question and answer sections or epilogue.

All lessons are transcribed from the original audio recordings of Jeshua (Jesus) who spoke through Jayem in order to bring forth *The Christ Mind Trilogy* and other aspects of *The Way of Mastery Pathway*. Reference by Jeshua to 'tapes' are reflective of the technology used at the time of the recordings.

To find out more about *The Way of Mastery Pathway,* or to read the precious sections not included within this edition please visit:

www.wayofmastery.com

The

WAY OF TRANSFORMATION
THE CHRIST MIND TRILOGY: VOLUME II

❧

Jeshua

The Way of Transformation

The Christ Mind Trilogy: Volume II

Jeshua

First Edition

WAY *of* MASTERY
www.wayofmastery.com

Published by:
PT. Heartfelt Publishing
PO Box 204, Ubud 80571
admin@wayofmastery.com
www.wayofmastery.com

ISBN: 978-602-9189-34-6

Jeshua Shares

I promise you this: If you become *wholly committed* to awakening from the dream you have dreamed since the stars first began to appear in the heavens, and even before that, if your one desire is to be only what God created . . . then lay at the altar of your heart with every breath, everything you *think* you know, everything you *think* you need, and look lovingly upon every place that fear has made a home in your mind, and allow correction to come. It will come. Regardless of how you experience it, it *will* come.

And the day and the moment will arise when all of your pain and fear and suffering will have vanished like a wind that pushes the foam of the wave away, revealing the clarity of the ocean beneath you. You will literally feel throughout your being that there never was a dream. Some memories will remain with you and you will know that somewhere you must've dreamed a dream or had a thought of wondering what it would be like to be other than the way God created you, but it will be such a faint echo that it will leave no trace upon you. In your heart you will smile gently, regardless of the circumstances in which you find yourself. There will be peace from the crown of the head to the tips of the toes, so to speak, and that peace will walk before you wherever you go. It will enter a room before you enter it with a body, and those who are becoming sensitive will wonder who has come into their place. And some will even say, "Behold, I believe Christ has come for dinner." And you will be that one, for that is who you are—Christ eternal.

~ The Early Years: Choose to See

Contents

Lesson One

Now, we begin.

And indeed, as always, greetings unto you, beloved and holy friends. As always, we come forth to join with you in this manner, through this voice. And yet, as always, we are not apart from where you are. And we are not inaccessible to any of God's Children. In Truth, and for the several thousandth time, I would say unto you that separation does not exist in all of Creation. This can only mean that I am not apart from where you are. And where you *are* has nothing at all to do with the location of the *body* that you have learned to call *your own.*

In Truth, you *are* Pure Spirit. In Truth, you are as I am. In Truth, that which you are abides throughout all dimensions of consciousness. In Truth, that which you are has *never* tasted separation from God. There is an aspect of you, yes indeed, that has chosen to *perceive* yourself as identified with the physical body in this third-dimensional world of yours called space and time. This is a part of the experience you have created and thus called to your *Self*. But, when I speak of Self, I speak not of the self which is the dream of the body, the self which is that which you've identified yourself with, but rather the Self that transcends all limitation and exists in all dimensions.

Beloved friends, by way of greeting, and by way of introduction to that which we will be speaking unto in this, your new year, by way of addressing what we have chosen to entitle *The Way of Transformation*, rest with this simple Truth: At no time are you imprisoned within the body. At no time—*at no time*—are you limited to the appearance that you have come to believe is you—no matter how deep the pain, no matter how certain you have been, what you call your common sense, telling you that,

I am here. I am this body.

This moment is happening. This is all there is.

Regardless of all of that, the Truth is not shaken. You are not the mere appearance of the body-mind that you have called the "self."

Now, with that simple point as a foundation, we can begin. Beloved friends, *The Way of Transformation* rests on exactly the same thing that all of your dreams rest upon—the *decision* concerning what *you* would be committed to. For you cannot dream a dream, that is, you cannot create an experience in the field of consciousness, without being one hundred percent committed to it. It may appear that this is not the case, but I assure you that it is.

This means that in each moment of your lived experience, what you are aware of is wholly uncaused by *anything* outside of yourself. For example, as we record these words, vibrated as thoughts through a physical body that you have come to have assigned to the one that you would call Jon Marc, as this process occurs there are a few present, currently hearing the vibrations created as these thoughts resonate through the mind, and then the brain, and then the vocal chords of *a* physical body, and it creates a sound pattern that resonates with the ears of certain other physical forms . . . Rest assured that if those

beings, those *fields of consciousness* that are hearing
these words, even as they are first recorded—if *they*
limit themselves to being only that body, receiving
certain frequencies of vibration touching their ears
and creating a certain neurological stimulus within
the brain and translating that vibration into certain
words of your English language, that experience is
not caused by anything outside themselves.

They are equally free, in this very moment (just as
you are, as you listen to what is called the 're-cording'
of these words), they are infinitely free to experience
this transmission of vibration in a wholly different
way, beyond what you call your English language.
They are free to perceive themselves from the realms
of Pure Spirit. They are free to see me, and those who
join with me, as we transmit this frequency which
creates the vibration through the physical form—just
as you are.

And therefore, by way of a simple exercise, for all of
you hearing these words, take just a moment, and
within your consciousness drop this simple pebble:

> *I am not what I have perceived myself to be. I am
> unlimited, Pure Spirit, and nothing is unavailable to
> me.*
>
> *Therefore, in this moment, I choose to open access to
> other dimensions of experience so that I might call this
> moment to me in a different way.*

And as the words are spoken, notice what images
begin to come into your field of awareness as you
perhaps imagine yourself to be far more than just

the body, abiding in far greater dimensions than the physical dimension. Do you see fleeting images of other beings, colors of light, subtle feelings that perhaps you hadn't been aware of while you are focusing on the *English translation* of the vibrations? What do you notice drifting through the field of your awareness? Pay attention to it, for you cannot imagine what you have not or are not experiencing.

You are the *field of consciousness* having that experience *now*. You create the capacity. You decide what will enter into the field of your awareness and how you will experience it. Beloved friends, learn to look beneath the scenes. Learn to feel beyond the body. Learn to allow yourself awareness of what steals across the metaphorical *corner of your eye*, that is, the *outer edges* of your field of awareness.

Come to realize that the experience you are most familiar with—that is, the one of being a body-mind, who listens to vibrations of sound, translates them into English and therefore perceives that you are having *a* conversation with *one* being who happens to be another body in space, sitting ten feet from you, or whose words are recorded upon a tape. Recognize that around the edges of that there is something far more vast, something which can be cultivated, that allows you to be aware at much more refined levels.

Eventually you will come to be able to perceive these dimensions of energy with your eyes open, as you look upon another body-mind who is currently having the experience of vibrating thoughts through it directed toward you—you call it a conversation. And you will see that other being, not as a body,

but as a field of light. You'll see colors. You'll feel
vibrations. And those colors and those vibrations will
tell you much more than the words could ever say to
you. The result, of course, is that you won't be fooled
by words nearly as often as you have been in the past.

Practice this little exercise as often as you choose,
in any and all circumstances. It is not difficult.
You simply use the field of your consciousness to
decide to be *aware* of what's around the edges of the
third-dimensional experience you are having. For
instance, when you pull in your automobile up to
what you call the red light, as you sit next to another
automobile with a driver, and you look over through
the physical eyes—if you limit yourself you will see
an automobile with another body sitting behind a
wheel, similar to what your body is doing (or what
you call your body).

What if you allowed yourself to play, by looking at
that being and saying within the mind,

> *This is but one small expression of that being. I
> wonder what's occurring around the edges?*

You might surprise yourself when suddenly a thought
comes into your consciousness. That thought, you
know, is not quite yours. It could be the thought of
the person in the car saying,

> *My God, I should have . . . why didn't I iron my
> husband's shirt this morning? Oh, he's going to be so
> angry!*

How many times have thoughts like that entered your
mind and you've dismissed them as imagination?

5

What we're suggesting here, is that you use the most ordinary moments of your day to become aware of your own being, your own naturally expanded, unlimited Self. There is nothing hidden at any time, and in any moment you have full access to the totality of another soul. Does that sound like an invasion of privacy? Beloved friends, there is no such thing. Privacy is important only for those who believe they are cut off, and separate, and perhaps have something to hide. In reality, *nothing* is hidden. And as you come to trust that the deep nature of your own being is perfect wisdom, perfect compassion, and perfect Love—you will begin to release the fear that you have built up around the *extraordinary* skills that you already possess.

You will discover that you can trust your unlimited Spirit. And as you sit in your car, looking at the one behind the wheel of the automobile next to you, and you allow yourself to relax and notice what's around the edges, as it touches your consciousness, you will realize that this means that minds are not separate, one from another. And if their mind is touching yours, yours is touching theirs, and you are free to send them Love. You are free to notice what you pick up from another and, without opening the physical mouth, you can send the answer of wisdom that they are seeking.

Imagine being able to go to your grocery store and push your little metal cart down the aisles so that you can fill it with the boxes of what appears to be fresh food, and notice the thought waves of those around you—beginning to pick up what's going on in their drama, their story, their life—and actually be able to (what your word would be) telepathically communicate to them the answers to their dilemmas. Would that not feel like a greater degree of freedom than what you are accustomed to?

You see, *The Way of Transformation* absolutely requires that you be *committed* to living differently. For is not transformation a change from the status quo? How can you experience transformation if you do not use time to *think* and *be* differently? Crying out to me will not do it. Reading a thousand holy books will not do it. One thing, and one thing only, will bring you into the transformation that you have sought—the *willingness* to abide where you are, *differently*.

Begin again with the simple exercise of reminding yourself that, in Truth, you are unlimited Spirit, abiding in all dimensions and all extraordinary abilities are already inherent in your consciousness—for if they were not, it would mean that God creates with *in*equality.

Well, you are born with that gift, but I don't have it.

No. God creates His beloved Son and the Sonship is made up of equals in Spirit. The only difference, in the field of time, is that it appears that some have accessed and cultivated their inherent abilities more so than have others.

You would then use this to perceive another as more *special* than you as a way of proving to yourself your lack of worth, your smallness, your weakness. Perhaps someday, if only you lived the next hundred lifetimes being a "good" person, then maybe these abilities will begin to spontaneously show up in you. But there are no accidents, and nothing you see being made manifest in the life of *anyone* has occurred by accident. Everything you see is *deliberate*—everything.

Therefore, if you would look upon my beloved brother, or the body that you have assigned to him, and say,

> *Oh, my goodness, he can talk with Jeshua, but I could never do that.*

Stop lying to yourself! Rather, come to see that if this ability is being made manifest in your field of awareness, it is because *you* have called it to *yourself* as a reminder of what is already inherent within *you*.

If another lays the hand of the body on the forehead of one who is sick, and the one who is sick arises and the disease is no longer present, remember that *you* have called that experience, through that beloved brother or sister, into the field of your consciousness to remind *you* of the Truth of your beingness. And if you feel attracted to being a healer, then drop everything else you are committed to and begin healing.

As we enter into this year of transformation, you will discover that we begin to speak more directly to you, in the sense of—what you call this—the "not beating about of the bush." Not placating your resistance, your fears, not stroking you for the dramas you have created that have *seemed* to separate you from the Truth of your divine nature. For as we move into *The*

Way of Transformation, the call is being sent from us to you—to arise and assume complete responsibility for all that you see, all that you think, and all that you choose. And rest assured, if you hear this call it is because a deeper part of you has called it to you as a way by which you remember that these things are already contained within you.

The *Way of Transformation* is the way of assuming responsibility for time, for each and every moment of it. For time is not a prison for you. It is that which flows out of your very consciousness, and there is never a place or a time—*never* a place or a time—which is more conducive to *The Way of Transformation* than the place in which you are and the time that is now. There is no one without *privilege*. There is no one by their station in life, as the world would see it, who is limited from watering and cultivating and bringing forth the fruit that rests within their unlimited consciousness. There is no one who is a victim of the world they see. For the world they see truly occurs nowhere save within the field of their awareness, which we call consciousness or mind. The buildings, the automobiles you drive, the dollars in the bank—none of that is real. These are merely symbols of the quality of experience you have chosen to call to yourself, as a temporary learning experience.

Beloved friends, use time well. Ask yourself,

> *Am I fully committed to transforming my awareness from one who has been sleeping, and perceiving myself as limited to the space and time dimension, or am I committed to truly hearing my brother's call to take up*

my cross and follow him?

That is, the cross of crucifixion, the heavy wooden cross that you've been carrying around that says,

> *Well, I'm really struggling and trying to get to Christed Consciousness, but . . . Oh, if, if I just, maybe if I got rid of my husband, that would do it. Or perhaps if I moved to another location, that would do it. Maybe there is a spiritual technique out there that I haven't found yet in the smorgasbord available. Once I find it and start practicing it, then I can get on with it.*

You are *in* the holiest of temples: your Self. You *abide* in the perfect moment for your transformation. Nothing limits you at all, or at any time. The power of the freedom of choice *is* the essence of Christ. And the very, very, very power that you have been using to try to convince yourself of your limitations is exactly the same power that I used to overcome death. There is no difference, except a wink of an eye, an intention, a commitment, a recognition—that is all. In reality, nothing is impossible to you and nothing unavailable to you.

So, what occurs, what occurs in the consciousness that seems to create the blockage, the obstacle to Love's presence? As you create a temporary perceived limitation as a way to call to you a certain quality of experience, there is a tendency to fall into the trap of identifying yourself with the constraints that you have set up, from your unlimited freedom, in order to have a temporary learning experience. When in your consciousness you come to be identified with the boundaries or the constraints—the lines upon the canvas that *you* have freely chosen to draw—you create an imprisonment. That imprisonment is actually a complete illusion, and in *reality* your unlimited Self goes on experiencing anything it wants, throughout all dimensions of Creation.

Your *belief* that you are defined by the lines you have drawn in the field of consciousness, the pebbles you have dropped, the ripples you have created—your belief that that is only you creates a constriction, and a density, and a conflict that is occurring nowhere in your being except in that part of you that has extended itself like a sunbeam from the sun into what you call your space-time dimension.

Now, think about this. If you feel constrained in this dimension, it does not mean that you *are* constrained. It simply means that one tiny ray of your Light is temporarily having a certain kind of experience. And if you trace that ray of Light back to its source, you find something brighter than ten thousand of your suns, something far more vast than the sun that lights your physical universe, something so vast that out of it has come forth a multitude of universes! That Light of your soul, Pure Spirit, remains undefiled and unlimited. That *tiny ray* can become aware of the whole, and that is the process of awakening. It doesn't really change anything at all, since you begin to become identified, not with the tiny little ray that's having a temporary experience, but that field out of which the very power to experience the space-time dimension is coming forth.

Imagine shifting your identity so that you are the ocean from which a multitude of waves are coming forth, and continually coming forth, each one slightly different, each one a little larger or smaller, a little faster, each one with a little more foam on it than the other—the very temporary, dancing waves being emitted from a field or an ocean of waters that knows neither beginning nor end and whose far shores can not be discovered. *That* is your Self, not the tiny wave that has a name and a history of being born at a certain time and living in a certain house or a city. It is certainly never what you call yourself as a banker, or a teacher, or a channel, or a mother, or a father. None of these things is what you are.

The Way of Transformation is much simpler than you think. But again, it rests on *your* decision to use time to be *wholly committed* to awakening from the narrow constraints you have placed upon your vast field of consciousness for no other reason than that it might be rather entertaining to allow this tiny little ray to continue in space and time for a while, while being aware of the totality of your Self and actually operating from that totality.

Can you imagine living like that? Can you imagine your body-mind driving its little automobile down the road, but every time you pull up to your red light and you notice someone next to you, you don't perceive . . . ? You will still see the automobile, you'll still see the body, but what you're feeling, what you are knowing, what you are seeing is that that is an *infinite field of consciousness*, just like you are, and that their mind field touches yours throughout all dimensions and that you are Christ, that you can transmit wisdom and Love to them.

You can learn to direct energies. You might see it as a certain color. You can touch their field, their auric field. You can send healing to the organs of the body that you can *see* are perhaps a little out of whack. *You* can be the embodiment in space and time of that Self that is so vast, so grand, so filled with extraordinary power, that all you can do is smile—perhaps unseen and unrecognized by those who, themselves, have become unwittingly identified with a little, tiny drop of foam which is part of the wave, which is part of the ocean of their Self.

But what they choose does not influence your choice. Listen very carefully again: What another chooses does not influence your choice at all, even when it seems like it. It isn't even accurate to say,

> *Oh well, I fell under the influence of so-and-so and so-and-so; I went a little unconscious, that's why it happened. I gave up myself.*

No. No. No! In every moment of your experience, what you experience is coming from *within* you. It is not placed in you from a source outside of yourself. And in every moment, you remain free to observe and to notice whether you are having a good time being where you are—that is, being in your perception of Life, and recognizing you have the power to think differently.

> *Oh, that's right, I'm not in a traffic jam. There is no such thing as a traffic jam. Everything is perfect. There is just a giant weaving together of experiences of infinite souls. So while I sit here in this little car with*

> *this funny little body, I'm going to be Christ. And I'm going to tap in to what's going on around the edges of my awareness. And I'll feel the thoughts of anyone I choose to direct attention to. And from the depth of my being, I will direct Love to them. I can choose to be the Truth of who I am. The red light, the automobiles, all jangled together—these things do not create my experience. My experience is flowing from within. It is being extended outward.*

Listen carefully. No one has the power to create your experience. No one has the power to limit your experience. And nowhere in the Laws of God has it ever been written that you must conform your experience to the choices of another. You remain free, to freely choose to be the embodiment of Christ. You are the one who can bless Creation. And it begins when you are willing to assume responsibility for what you want to use time for.

In Truth, you're doing it anyway. You are always using time for exactly what *you* are choosing. You're not surviving. You're not trying to get things done that the world is requiring. Never is anything occurring except that you are having awareness of the effects of how you are choosing to use consciousness, and that's all.

Here is where *The Way of Transformation* begins. Ultimately, it is also where it ends. But the difference will be that you will no longer even want to choose anything that speaks of limitation. Even though the body-mind, that you once identified as yourself, still seems to be moving about in space and time, you won't even look at that body-mind and say 'mine. '

You will simply say,

> *The body-mind—a temporary communication device brought forth from the ocean of my unlimited Self as I have done a multitude of times in a multitude of universes—what's the big deal?*

Your consciousness will literally *shift*. It will take a new perspective. And you will know that you are Pure Spirit, that you do not abide in time at all, that you can simply delight in utilizing the body-mind as a communication device.

When you get on your airplane and you travel to some distant shore to a place that you are enjoying being in, you are still using the body-mind as a communication device between you and the Earth, between you and other creations that have come forth from other minds, whether it be a beautiful building or a beautiful painting. All that you are ever experiencing is something that you have drawn to yourself through the medium of the body—an experience, and that is all. You are the unlimited one who's in the driver's seat.

The second stage, closely related to the first that we described to you earlier in *The Way of Transformation*, requires that you begin to bring awareness to the little squiggly lines that you have drawn on the white and unlimited and perfectly unblemished canvas of consciousness. Some would call this—your psychologists would call these *personalities* or masks. Come to be aware of the *little selves* you have created. Begin to ask yourself,

What am I defending? What am I continuing on a daily basis that no longer fulfills me? After all, I've been there. I have done that. How might I look upon these little selves, these little drops of foam on this temporary wave I've brought forth? How might I use them differently? I wonder if I could create a brand new one?

Why is this important? It is because the squiggles you have drawn—perhaps you would say to yourself,

> *Well, I am Mary Jane. I am a vice president at a bank. I was born in such and such a city. My parents are so-and-so and so-and-so, and I'd really be different except my sister used to beat me when I was young.*

—the second you define yourself, you constrain yourself within the parameters that you have chosen to value. And you, [snaps fingers] that quickly, create exactly the experience of the vibrations that are the effect of the squiggles. Think of those squiggles, the parameters of a little self, as the effect of certain pebbles that have been dropped into the pond of your consciousness. Once you draw the lines, certain effects flow from it.

What if you were to decide to create a self that sees itself as perfectly unlimited? And instead of saying,

> *Well, I have to go see my sister. I know she used to beat me, but that's the way it is. It's just who I am,*

you simply sat back and said,

> *You know, I'm a perfectly unlimited being, and I think I'll create a self who is an expression of the unlimited*

Love of Christ. And I'm going to go see this human being (you might use their name but not to call them your sister)—I'm going to go see this being and I'm going to utilize time for beaming as much Love to them as I can, for no other reason than it will feel rather grand to do so. I am the embodiment of Christ, and this one may not know it, but that doesn't matter. I can enjoy it anyway.

Do you see how that could begin to move you beyond an identification of a certain definition of yourself that has actually locked you in to a narrow parameter, or set of parameters, which can only have certain kinds of effects? What if you were to sit down with those you call your parents and deliberately chose to look at them as beings that *you* had called to your field of awareness, that they are infinite and free beings in perfect equality with you? And they simply chose to receive your cosmic telegram and took on a certain role in space and time to help you play out what *you* wanted to learn. Would that begin to shift your identification with them as merely parents? For if you look upon them and say,

Those are my parents,

you have defined yourself as *only* their child. Do you begin to see the significance?

'Tis very, very important to bring awareness to the definitions you have given yourself, and keep insisting upon, each and every day. That is like dropping the same pebble into the same stream, creating the same effects—and nothing is transformed.

It also brings up some fear.

> *What would happen if I let go of the definitions that I'm familiar with?*

And here's the answer: Nothing will happen, because in reality those definitions have never truly limited your unlimited Self from going on creating and experiencing, throughout all dimensions. The only change that could be said to occur, is that that little tiny ray of your beingness that is currently dancing through the experience of being a mind-body in space and time, will begin to throw open the doors and actually access Cosmic Awareness.

If you want the experience of walking on this planet as an enlightened master, first come to understand the foundation upon which *The Way of Transformation* is based. Secondly, bring awareness to the definitions of your self that have become unconscious for you. And then *deliberately redefine* your self as you enter into the field of your experiences. Does that make sense for you?

And here is the nub: No one can make the decision for you.

I have never enlightened anyone. I have never even so much as lifted them an inch. I have merely chosen to demonstrate unlimitedness for myself, and part of that experience was taking on the crucifixion, just so that I could learn how to overcome death. That was *my* choice, *my* pathway, *my* calling forth of experience. I can tell you that it's much more grand to be in the body while being completely aware of your Cosmic

18

Self. And in the same moment, I must say to you, it's perfectly okay for you to perceive yourself as a limited ray of consciousness. Yes, there are certain results that follow. But still, you are completely free to continue in that field of experience for as long as you wish.

Imagine one who goes to swim in the waters of what you call a pool, and there are certain parameters—each end may be forty of your feet in length and the sides might be two hundred feet in length; it doesn't matter. There is still a certain volume of water, and that is the field in which you swim. That field of water is like the field of your consciousness. It is shaped by the boundaries that *you* choose to draw. The very same being could say,

> *I am much too grand to swim in a pool. I believe I'll put the little body on an airplane and fly to the grand ocean—there to swim in the midst, unbounded by a box.*

The experience of *that* swimming is much different.

Your consciousness is exactly like that. And all that you experience, from the moment you awaken in the morning until the moment you awaken in the morning again (because there is no downtime)—everything you see, everything you experience, is the *direct result* of where and how you have drawn the lines on the blank canvas of consciousness. And you are free at any time to erase them and draw differently.

Never say, then, that you have discovered something. Rather, learn to say,

I am experiencing the effects of certain lines I have drawn in the infinite field of my beingness. And you know something? They are perfectly okay.

That is, taking a walk in the rain—learn to enjoy it, from the place of unlimitedness within you, as a Christ would walk upon this Earth and say,

I choose to feel the rain upon the skin of this body. I feel the shiver of the flesh against the cold. What a delight it is! I am unlimited, forever! And this moment does not define me. It does not imprison me. I am free! I am free!

Tomorrow, I might move to some warmer climate where the sun shines and there are no clouds of rain. And if so, I will enjoy the rays of the sunlight upon my skin and the sweat upon the brow. And I will notice what it feels like as it trickles across the skin—not my skin, but the skin.

And when I meet a friend, I will remind myself that our fields of mind are meeting in many dimensions. What will I choose to bring to that moment? Will I see myself as limited to the boundaries of the skin of the body? Will I only tell them of all my laments? "My car had a flat tire, and then my mommy called and she's unhappy because I forgot her birthday, and oh, my goodness, I don't know how I'm going to get through." Or, am I going to meet them as the unlimited Cosmic Being that I am?

Will I create the space in which I get to enjoy beaming Love to them? Will I enjoy seeing what's occurring just around the edges of the third-dimensional experience that, of course, does go on? "Hello Fred, nice to see

*you." But around the corners, "Oh, Fred, you had
an argument with your wife. Let me talk to you
about that," without ever opening the physical mouth.
"Here's some Love for you. You know the wisdom.
You know the answer." Hmm . . . Oh, a little cancer
beginning to form in the colon. I think I'll send light
to it. "Yes, yes, so how's the wife, how are the children?
Oh, very good." Light beaming into the cancer, light
beaming into the cancer.*

Which experience do you prefer: the contracted
awareness within two small squiggles on an infinite
canvas of Radiant Light, or the Radiant Light Itself,
operating *through* very temporary and freely chosen
'squiggles' called the body-mind?

The Way of Transformation begins with you deciding
what you are most committed to. It requires bringing
awareness to every set of definitions you have
adopted about the self and placed as an overlay upon
it. It culminates in the *transparency* of the body-mind
self, the little ray of light that you think you are, so
that even while that continues for a little while, it is
permeated by an awareness of your Cosmic Being.
And that becomes your identity.

And you are Christ, playing in the world—unlimited,
unfettered, unvictimized by anything. And what
arises, arises, and what passes away, passes away. And
arising and passing away are exactly the same to you.
Love comes; it is received. Love *seems* to be taken; so
what? You bless the being that withdraws awareness
from you and you simply open to whoever comes
into your consciousness. For you decide how you will
be in relationship with each moment. And you never

discover something *out there* that's *right*. You simply create the structure of your experience.

Whenever another says to you,

> *Well, I like to eat meat. I love it raw and bloody upon my plate,*

and you've been eating nothing but fruits and vegetables, there is no reason to say anything at all. Just smile, decide that you can beam them Love—not because they're doing something wrong and if you love them they might change—but because their decision doesn't mean anything. It is just a description of how they are structuring their experience. If you identify with yourself as a 'pure vegetarian,' you will not be able to prevent yourself from judging your brother or sister. And where judgment abides, you have created separation, and for a moment you lose the presence of Love.

Can you become selfish enough to learn to truly recognize that you are not influenced by anyone else's choices, and their choices do not say anything about your own? You are free to embrace your experience as being wholly Self-created out of perfect innocence, perfect playfulness, the free use of time to generate experience. Hmm.

Much has been given to you already in this time, what you call this recording. We would highly suggest for those *committed* to transformation, that they go back and be very clear about what is being shared. Begin this year to create your own personal transformation journal. Let it be used for no other purpose.

Take the journal and find a picture that represents
for you the highest. the deepest, the most passionate,
the most beautiful expression of *Love* that you can
imagine. Don't compare it to anybody else's. Just put
it on the front of the journal. Buy a pen that will be
used for no other reason than this. Find a place to
place this journal so that nothing else occupies that
space, whether it be on your altar, in a drawer by your
bed. Find a place, deliberately, out of the field of your
Christedness, and say,

Ah, this is the place.

Then, each time you receive one of these tapes,
go through it carefully and write down the key
points that are being shared. And decide what they
will mean for you. And decide what steps you will
take to incorporate them into your lived, daily
experience—even if that means that they are not
going to be incorporated at all. Take one hundred
percent responsibility for the decision and write
down in your journal,

*I don't think I'm going to do that. I own it; I decide
freely. That's the way it is.*

As you do this, by the time the year ends, you will be
surprised at what you have written in your journal.
As you go through it month by month, also keep
track of some of the things that you experience as
you play with the practices that we give you. How
are things changing? What experiences are you
beginning to have as you explore the space just
beyond the corners of your normal awareness? When
you do the exercise we suggested when we began,

what images came, what thoughts did you notice, what colors did you see? Write them down, jot them down. Have fun with it.

For indeed, in each month we will be giving you very specific, though what may seem as very simple exercises. But they are designed to give you access to what is already occurring at all times, in a way that can foster and deepen your *deliberate awareness* of what is occurring all the time: your cosmic and unlimited Self.

The only transformation you can experience in space and time is the reaching down from the depth of the ocean into one tiny, temporary wave and re-adjusting the little foam drops on the tip of the wave you call the body-mind of the self, so that it begins to be a transparent conduit for an awareness of the ocean itself. That's the game of awakening. It is actually the most delightful use of time you will ever find.

And as you choose to do that, trust me, it will carry you beyond this world—not from denial, but simply because you've outgrown it. And there are dimensions of experience awaiting you that are so much more grand than the dimension of the body-mind. But the way that you get to them is by bringing *full awareness* to what you are choosing to experience in each and every moment. Soap on the skin in the morning shower—wow, how amazing! Raindrop upon the cheek. Shiver against the cold. The sound of a cat meowing. The thoughts of a dog across the street. These things you call to yourself in this dimension.

Don't you want to taste it all? Don't you want to wrap yourself around it all? Don't you want to remember that magic is around you? And that out of magic, the moment you are experiencing is being created from within *your* Holy Self. It's never been, and it will never be again—Mystery of all mysteries, Dance of Creation, Reality of Love! There is no higher state in the mind-body than to live as one who's been *blown away* and lives in that state perpetually. Then you are free and the world has no hold upon you.

So, here we will come to the end of this hour's message. 'Tis a beginning for anyone who chooses to wrap their unlimited hands around it. But alas, we cannot shape the use of it for you. And if you don't like where you are, look no further than yourself.

We await you. We will reach out for you, in a million different ways, across space and time into the space between your thoughts—not just through the mechanism of this tape, but every time there is a little space open in your consciousness. Indeed, we will come and whisper,

> *Beloved friend, come and play at a vaster level. It is all within you. Come and play. Come and play with God's Children!*

You are free. In this moment, you are as free as you will ever be, right now.

How, then, will you use time?

What will you construct out of your infinite field of awareness? What world will you look upon? What thoughts will you think? What feelings will you

25

evoke within the cells? Where will you direct the body to be plopped down on a daily basis? How will you observe, or how will you enter into, relationship with each moment—whether touching a dial, or touching a body? It really makes no difference. What will you bring to that experience? Is it Christ touching the shoulder of another, or is it just some limited, needy self?

Who will you say that you are to this world? For what you decree *is*, [snaps fingers] instantly. There's no way out of this responsibility. Stop fighting it and birth Christ where once you thought something less than that has dwelt.

Beloved friends, peace be unto you always, and always I am with you. And I come to you not alone, but with many who have delighted in creating a resonance with me, and I with them, for no other reason than that power expands *exponentially* when minds join in Love from a foundation of wholeness and not neediness. I do not need the one that you call my Mother; she does not need me. But, oh, how we delight in creating *together* that which extends the holy, the good, and the beautiful—without end! Will you come and play with us?

Peace, then, be unto you always. And, as always,

Amen.

Lesson Two

Now, we begin.

And indeed, once again, greetings unto you, beloved and holy friends. We would trust, then, that this moment finds you well. We would trust, then, that this moment finds you willing to be wholly where you are. We would trust, then, that in this moment, we would find you willing to assume responsibility for the choices you have made, that have literally created the environment that you are experiencing in this moment: the chair in which you sit, the walls around you, the things that hang upon the walls, the individuals with whom you find yourself in close proximity, the individuals with whom you find yourself in relationship, the individuals with whom you work, those with whom you play, those with whom you share. We would trust that *this moment* finds *you*, the Holy Child of God, at play in the Kingdom of Christ.

And if not . . . if, as you listen to that greeting, you are aware within yourself that,

> *Well, that's not quite the perspective from which I was beginning my listening of this tape. I thought I was going to sit down and listen to Christ.*

If there be some element, some touch, some trace within you of that perspective, then pause the tape right now. And, as you do so, abide by yourself, and take several deep breaths, if you wish. Go back to the five minute exercise of simply being the presence of Christ. For well do we perceive that many of you have already forgotten that the exercise exists.

At the end of the five minutes, simply remind yourself that what is true always, is always true: *Only Love is Real.* And what is Real cannot be threatened by what does not truly exist. And in each moment in which your perceptions are less than flowing from the remembrance of who you are, you have been *in* unreality. When you notice this, take the *time* and use it constructively, by returning to the Truth. So, pause the tape if you must—we'll be going nowhere—and return in five minutes.

Now, *The Way of Transformation* is simple, for the way of efforting one's way into the Kingdom cannot flow from the guidance of the Holy Spirit. For where there is effort, there is a separate will, called the ego, that believes itself to be (and would love to convince you of this), believes itself to be small, powerless, and *knows* that it is pervaded by fear. Love requires no effort, only the little willingness necessary to *allow it* to flow from the depth of your being, through you, that it might be extended throughout Creation.

Beloved friends, *The Way of Transformation*, again, requires only that you extend to yourself the willingness necessary to put into practice using time *differently*. No, it doesn't mean that you have to quit your job and go live in a little hut on top of a mountain somewhere. You would not *necessarily* use time differently by doing so. It *does* require that you begin with the simple recognition that there can be no set of *perceived* circumstances that truly have the power to separate you from your God. No set of circumstances, no set of relationships—not the weather, not the amount of money that you are allowing yourself to receive for the expenditure of your time—there is *nothing* in the world that has the power to separate you from your God.

You are the one who holds dominion over all things. And what does this idea of dominion mean? It means that *you* are the one who is the source of the power which can choose how you will see what is around you, how you will perceive it, what you will believe most about it. *You* are the one with the power to penetrate the illusory veil of the world and see the Heart, or the Essence, or the Truth, or the Christ Child in everything—a blade of grass, the cry of a child, the barking of a dog, the coming of the mail with the bills. Hmm.

Therefore, *The Way of Transformation* does not require you to change your circumstances. It merely requires that you change *your attitude* toward them, by recognizing that they are harmless, by recognizing that *you* have called all things to yourself.

There are many that would teach that you must sit around and ponder why you did this, and why you did that, and . . . oh, my goodness gracious! I say unto you, all that is required to begin is the willingness to accept that in the great mystery of consciousness, *you* are the power and the source for all that you think, all that you see, all that you feel, and all that you would be and do. You abide in that freedom *constantly*.

The Way of Transformation, then, rests simply on that:

> *How will I decide to use my time? Finding myself here in this moment, can I remember that I am free to see*

things differently? I am free to look lovingly upon the world. I do not need to wait for something outside of myself to create a stimulus that elicits a loving response.

You don't need to wait for your mate to come and give you the hug that you want so much. You don't need to wait until your mother calls you on the phone and begs for your forgiveness for how cruelly she treated you when you were growing up. You don't need to wait until President Clinton is no longer in the White House. You don't need to wait for the great contest that comes in the mail that brings you millions of dollars. You don't need to wait for that to happen. Right now, you are the one that is free.

But perhaps you have imprisoned yourself, by waiting for Love to show up outside of you to trigger a response within you, when you feel it or recognize it, so that finally you feel loving. Those that know aloneness are not limited in extending Love. And those that know loneliness yet retain the power to make the decision *to love*. It can never be taken from you.

So, here is a simple exercise that we would wish to give you. When next you find yourself alone and perhaps feeling just a little lonely, and you notice that the mind is spinning with thoughts, and you are feeling perhaps just a little weak and out of sorts—pick up what you call your telephone book. Take three deep breaths, and with each breath say to yourself,

In Reality, I remain as I am created to be.
I am the Holy Child of God.

Then merely open the phone book. Place your hand on one of the pages with the many names and numbers and just *feel* your way to a specific name and number (and you'll know the feeling). And then, for the fun of it, call that person. And when they answer the phone, merely say,

> *I'm not here to sell you anything, I just need about fifteen seconds of your time. I know you've never met me, but I was just sitting in my chair remembering that the Truth is true always. And I'm calling to remind you that you are loved by God! You've never failed. You've never done anything wrong. You remain pure and innocent, even now. And I just wanted to give my blessings to you. Have a nice day. Good-bye.*

For you see, the world in which you live has but one purpose. It is the *same* purpose that all dimensions of Creation have: to be the extension of the Father's Love. For that is what Creation is. And then, to *extend* that Love from that world, from that dimension. Each and every one of you has but one treasure, *only one treasure*. It is not your child. It is not your spouse. It is not the new car in the garage. Your treasure is your Reality as the *unlimited, holy and only begotten Child of God*. You are a *field of consciousness* through which the Father would extend *Himself*.

This means that if this is your only treasure, your greatest joy will be discovered as you cultivate within yourself the *habits of mind*, the *habits of body*, the *habits of choice*, that begin to align what you think, what you see, and what you do with the Truth that is true always. For your joy will be found as you recognize that you exist to extend your treasure. And as you

31

do so, you immediately add to your Father's treasure, Whose only will is to extend That Which He Is, forever—unbounded, unlimited. And *God is but Love*.

Now, the grand thing about Love is this: *It* does not require any set of conditions to exist before *It* does. Now, how is this different than some of the things you experience in life? Rest assured that, as a body, there are certain conditions that must exist before the body can be satiated with food or water. There must be certain conditions that are met before the body stops shivering against the cold. Your world is based on the topsy-turvy perception (that is an interesting word, by the way, topsy-turvy... hmm), is based on the perception that conditions must be met *before* there can be a choice for peace instead of war, for forgiveness instead of judgment, for Love instead of fear.

> *And when the conditions outside of me change, then I'll make the choice for Love.*

I have often said that the world is merely the reflection of the insane choice to deny Love and to be devoted to fear. The world is diametrically opposed to the Truth of the Kingdom. The world is the opposite of Reality. *The Way of Transformation*, then, rests on the complete reversal of the thought system you have learned in the world. But that thought system is not merely the practice of new ideas, repeated *ad nauseum* in the mind. That reversal of thought must *permeate* the entire field of the body-mind (which is nothing more than the field of your consciousness), so that you *know* that change has occurred.

So that when you are in any set of circumstances that once seemed to elicit judgment, or fear, or anger, or hurt, or sadness, that you recognize,

> *My goodness, my whole body feels different. I just feel like being loving. I feel totally safe. What's the big deal here? Oh, I remember when these kinds of circumstances would have elicited sadness, or hurt, or fear, or anger—and now, I just think it's a beautiful place to be. Because, here I can extend the Love of Christ. Wow, what a joy! What a treasure! Thank God, I have this moment in which I can be the blessing that blesses this world.*

And what is the world, if not each moment of relationship in which you find yourself?

So, beloved friends, *the use of time is pivotal.* The use of time *determines*, at all levels, what you will experience in your tomorrows. And long after the body ceases to be the teaching and learning device that you are most attached to, long after the body dies, you will, indeed, be continually stepping into your tomorrows. For you are that sunbeam sent forth from the sun, from the Mind of God. And that Light never stops traveling—let's put it that way, to use a spatial term. You will never cease to create. You will never cease to experience.

The only choice you ever have is this:

> *Will I assume responsibility for doing whatever I must do to eradicate every misperception, every obstacle to the presence of Love, every limited belief I have ever learned about anyone or anything—especially about*

> *myself? When will I choose to assume responsibility for cultivating that perfect remembrance that I and my Father are One—that I can perceive the real world?*

. . . the reality that shines through everything . . . that is present in the very material that makes up the chair in which you are sitting . . . that literally pervades the thing that you call the body that you think is so dense and hard. Or perhaps, if you have not been exercising, it is also a little soft.

The point is, there is *nothing* that you see that is not pervaded by the Perfect Radiance of God's Holy Presence—*nothing.* The stone, a leaf, a piece of paper blown by the wind, even the shoutings of fear and anger from anyone yet contains within it—if you would receive it—the Perfect Love of God. For your Father does not ever recoil or withdraw from the unlimited and perfect Extension of Himself. And God is but Love. And if you did not abide *wholly* in that Love in this moment, you would immediately cease to exist. I don't just mean die; I mean, literally, *cease to exist.* There would be no trace of thought, or memory in any mind, of you. It is only because Love *Is* that You *Are.*

This is why I once said,

> *Of myself I can do nothing, but my Father, through me, does these things.*

I did not say,

> *I learned these of my Father, and now I will be the maker and doer.*

I acknowledged my complete helplessness, my complete dependency. I eradicated any perception that I was a self separate from God. I stopped giving authority to the tiny, little gnat shouting at the vastness of space,

My *will be done!*

As you sit in your chair, then, in this moment—hopefully with your Transformation Journal in your lap, and the pen that you have purchased for only this purpose remember this: You are *wholly dependent* at all times on the pervasive Reality of Love, which has given you existence out of Its desire to extend Its treasure—joy. This is the reality of who you are in this moment. You are as the wave that has arisen from the Ocean of God's perfect and holy Love. You could not for a moment be cut off from it. And yes, tomorrow things will change. Yes, there will be a point when the body breaks down and dies. Yes, there will be a moment in which all that you see before you will be there no longer, for all things that arise in time, end in time. That's the way it is. And yet, *you* are free to cultivate the ability to perceive the *real* world—to see, to know, to feel, to taste, to be, to extend That which is Real. And only Love meets that definition.

Therefore, again, by way of another exercise, take just a moment. And if the eyes are closed, open them and look around you. What is the first thing that your eyes see? Be with it. Don't be so fast to judge it as a candle, or a flower, or a picture. Simply be with it. Let the body relax. Stop thinking so much.

What is this thing? Do you truly know what it is, or what it's for? You describe it, you name it, as Adam once did the animals in the story of the Garden of Eden. And the human mind believes that once it has named or defined a thing, it therefore *knows* it. It is called the *smugness of egoic knowledge*.

But do you *truly* know what that thing is? Do you recognize what has come about to even bring it into existence? How many minds had to have been involved in bringing forth that creation? What are the materials it is made out of? Where did the materials come from? What plant, what rock, what metal has been discovered and extracted from the body of the Earth to become that shape? How on earth did that happen? Where did the very molecules and atoms come from? What *is* that thing that I am looking at?

Can you find a place in which you merely rest in *awe*, and recognize your complete ignorance? You did not make that thing. You cannot find the moment in which that thing first began to arise as a thought in someone's mind. You are completely unaware of the moment of the birthing of the substance from which that object has been created. Look at it, then, with awe, and recognize that it has come forth from the same place as you—mystery; utter, sheer mystery. Do you not then feel an affinity with it? Are you not in relationship with it? Can you not, then, begin to sense the *sacredness* in which that relationship abides? For mystery *is* sacred, and it transcends even the greatest of minds. The greatest of philosophers can not comprehend the *field of mystery* in which all relationships arise.

And now, looking upon that object, whatever it is, recognize that you have called it into relationship with yourself. Ponder for a moment, and consider,

> *Out of what vibration of consciousness did I first call this object to myself?*

You might remember purchasing it in a store. See if you can discover the very first moment in your memory, in your consciousness, in which this object came into the field of your awareness. What was going on? What were you thinking, or were you thinking at all? What motivated you to bring it into the field of your home? If you are at a friend's house, the question remains the same. What motivated you to be where you are right now? What choices were you making with consciousness?

Now, again, we would suggest that you pause the tape and spend about five minutes repeating this exercise with several objects or things that you see in the room around you. Don't forget that that might even include your kneecap, or your hand, a ring upon your finger, the socks upon the feet. Enjoy this exercise. But remember, don't press the brain; that is, don't think so hard. Relax the body. Sit in the chair as though you were Christ and just look, and go through the kinds of questions we've given unto you. And then we will continue . . .

So, how did that go? Beloved friends, this exercise is very, very similar to one that I was also given by my Essene teachers when I was fairly young. And I would spend hours—*hours*—not just five minutes, but literally hours doing this exercise. I would do it in my father's house. I would do it in the synagogues. I would do it in the streets of the villages. My favorite time and place to do it was just at dusk, as the sun would begin to set. And as it did so, and I observed the colors, and felt the changes in the temperature of the air upon my skin, as I looked at the breezes dancing across the grasses, as I heard the song of the bird, I would be with these things, just as I just asked you to be with the objects in your room. And hours would go by, as I would sit and try to look at each and every star in the sky, asking myself the same questions:

> *Can I discover the source of this that I am seeing? Where did it come from? How could it be? What has brought this forth?*

And as I began to sense that I was calling these things into my experience, I began to discern what brought me *true joy*—not just a moment of pleasure, or satisfaction, or sense of security, but that which elicited *true joy*. And I discovered that what always brought joy was when I was willing to surrender into the *awe of mystery*, to penetrate the thoughts, and perceptions, and attitudes, and definitions that the world had taught me. To look at a plate, and not just see a plate, but to see mystery unfolding before me. To sit and look at a star. To sit and look at a sacred text. To sit and look at one diseased, who sits at the side of the road covered with dust, and *to see no difference*—to see them pervaded by the same Mystery, the presence of my Father's Love. I began to sense that that Love pervaded me, that the very body-mind that I thought had been me, Jeshua ben Joseph,

was arising out of Mystery . . . out of Mystery . . . out
of Mystery . . . that *I did not create myself!* And I finally
came to realize that even I, Jeshua ben Joseph, was a
Mystery with which I was in relationship.

And I decided to be in relationship with my own self,
what we refer to as the body-mind, that peculiar sense
of awareness in which you say, "I am." I decided to
be in relationship with the *totality* of my Self—mind,
spirit, soul, emotion, body—with the same sense
of awe and mystery that I felt when I looked upon
the farthest of stars deep into the night on a quiet
hillside. *And that changed everything.* I gave up my self-
definitions. I did not see myself as a carpenter's son. I
did not see myself as a Jew. I no longer saw myself as
a student of the Essenes.

I came to see my Self as the mysterious extension of
something beyond my comprehension. I saw my Self
as a sunbeam to the sun. I saw my Self as the very
mystery of God's presence being unfolded in the
realm of manifestation. I saw that all that I thought,
even down to the body, was temporary; that it was
an ongoing foreverness; that whatever it was that was
birthing me was *eternal*, and that if I could just *rest* in
That, if I could *abide* with That, if I could *return* to
That—even prior to every breath—that I could tap
into the very Power of Creation Itself. And get out
of the way, and get out of the way, and get out of
the way. And keep diving deeper into Mystery upon
Mystery upon Mystery.

I never let my mind rest from that day. I never
once decided I was done. I never defended a single

perception that I held about anyone or anything. And I cultivated over time, by using time wisely—I cultivated the willingness and the ability to seek first the Kingdom, even to the point where I was doing it *prior* to every word spoken, every gesture made with the body:

> *Father, I rest in You. What would You live through me in this moment? Let me witness it! Let me feel it! Let me taste it! Take me ever deeper into Your mystery. I want all of You!*

And if I might make a confession, that has never ended. I am still saying,

> *Father, I want all of You!*

The Way of Transformation—the willingness to use time differently. There must come a point in the journey of each individual in which the head bows, and the thought emerges,

> *I want only God, and I no longer care what it takes, what is required. I submit to the Mysterious Force that is Life, asking only that I be transformed into the perfect Field of Awareness through which that Love flows without obstruction.*

Now, what you will discover, in the end, is that the only obstruction is fear, and some expression of it. And each time you begin to set aside fear, and choose to bless the world from the perfect holiness of your union with God—each time you *dare* to be so arrogant in the eyes of the world as to be the presence of Christ, each time you relax the mind and the body and recognize,

> *Of myself I do nothing. Something is living me, and it is to That which I surrender,*

you will cultivate a way of being in the world that is not here. That is, it is not within the perceptual mode that makes up the world.

You will be different. You will look the same, but *you* will not be the you that the world has known. You will speak as you've always spoken. You'll know your social security number. However, there will be a definite sense that you live, yet not you, but *That One* is living you. And somehow, inextricably, unexplainably, you are being allowed to be the Field of Awareness that gets to witness Life living as you. And you will know that it is sacred. You will know that it is beautiful—that right now, wherever you are in this moment, *you* are the embodiment and the expression of Mystery: Love forever extending Itself. You are the very Joy of God!

And you will continue to be so throughout all of existence. There will never be a time when you will cease to be. But by choosing to surrender defense of the perceptions you have come to identify as *you*, by choosing to release the *grip* on the fears you believe are justified, the judgments that you believe are true, as you surrender your grip on the world you have made, Creation will flow through you:

> *Of myself, I do nothing. I merely witness the flow of Love through me. And I have used time wisely to cultivate perfect remembrance of the real world. Time*

and space do not imprison me. This body is not me. I use it as a tool to fashion and shape that which, in this world, can extend Love into any moment.

And so, we have come, now, to a good ending point for this, our second adventure into *The Way of Transformation.* Again, notice what thoughts, what pictures, what items you have chosen to write into your journal. Notice the feelings that are occurring in the body, even now. Notice the thoughts, the pictures, the images that you may hear echoing through the field of the mind. You abide nowhere but in the infinitude of God's presence. And mastery comes when finally you choose to release all attachment to fear. And in perfect surrender you release the dream of the dreamer itself, and *allow the Mystery of Life to live you*—without obstruction, without fear, in perfect knowledge that,

I and my Father are One. There is nothing I have to do to get God. *There are only some things to be released, so that* God can get me.

And so, beloved friends, heed well what was shared, at times in a very subtle way, in this hour. We would *highly* suggest that you listen to this tape several times, in different environments, at different times—perhaps at three in the morning, perhaps at midnight. As your spring comes to warm the Earth, again, take this tape and find a small hill where you can gaze at the stars, and perhaps, abide with them differently.

Listen to this tape when you're feeling harried or stressed. Look at all of the different sets of circumstances that you have believed have the power to limit your choice or distract your energy. And listen to this tape in those circumstances—when you're sad, when you're lonely, when you're harried, when the room is filled with fifty thousand friends (well, okay, perhaps ten or fifteen will do). Take it and listen to it sitting on a park bench, on what you call the benches in the great malls where the many beings in your country come to worship their god of "stuff," and exchange their golden coins for it—you call it the "shopping." And shop instead for a new quality of awareness, a new way of being—that which penetrates what you believe you're seeing, and reveals to you the perfect harmony of the Kingdom, the presence of the Love of God.

No one will ever make this journey for you. No one you see, no one with whom you live, will ever make the journey to God *for you.* So get clear about your priorities, and seek first the Kingdom. And above all, know that you are not alone. We are, indeed, with you always. And I close, then, by saying,

I love you.

Peace, then, be unto you always.

Amen.

Lesson Three

Now, we begin.

And, indeed, once again greetings unto you, beloved and holy friends. We come forth again with *great joy* to abide with you, to communicate with you in this manner, which is but only one way in which we come to share our thoughts with you, through which we come to share our Love for you, through which we come to abide with you, in celebration that we are but one Mind and one Heart, for those who choose to release all illusions and journey to the Heart of God. And there can only be Oneness, brotherhood, sisterhood, eternally. There can only be one purpose and one goal. There can only be Christ expressing the Mind of God.

Therefore, indeed, it is with great joy that we have come forth to abide with you in this hour. And we would ask you to set aside the roar and din of the world, to simply hold the thought in the mind, for just the briefest of moments, that right now you need not be concerned for anything, that the world you have dreamt into being, simply to experience it, can be placed upon a shelf . . . that in this hour there is simply this experience: your willingness to prepare a place for us and to hear subtle vibrations, translated as thoughts, shaping the form of the vocal cords, to utter the words in the English language that can direct the heart toward the soul, that can direct the soul toward the spirit, that can direct the spirit into *awakening fully* as the presence of the *Thought of Love in form*. For this is what you are made to be. And this is what you *are* eternally, regardless of the vibrations of thoughts that

44

you allow to make a home in your mind, temporarily.

You have a term in your legal system—temporary insanity.

My client is not guilty, it was just temporary insanity.

Rest assured, beloved friend, that that is exactly how it is in the cosmic dimensions of your being. Your Father knows that given perfectly free will, you have elected at times to be temporarily insane. Knowing this, no judgment has been passed, and you have never been made wrong by your Creator.

And you have never failed to create and attract *precisely* those most beautiful lessons that have triggered for you what you most need to learn, what you most need to feel. And in each moment you exist in an exquisite perfection of your own making, your own collaboration with one another. You therefore, my beloved friends, are already as I am. And we merely work together to restore to your mind what God has placed there since before the beginning of time. We work together in joy and in innocence and in perfect simplicity to *re-call*, to *re-member*, what is true always, and then to explore the expansion of that Truth beyond the boundaries of every fearful thought, beyond the limitations of every egoic perception, beyond even the body, itself, which can be only a temporary communication device usable only within the very thin slice of Creation that you call the physical world.

Beloved friends, *The Way of Transformation* does, indeed, require your commitment. And where you feel that your commitment has wavered, when you become aware of it, simply choose anew. And the end of the journey must be perfectly certain. For as you have created your journey away from God, in your imagination, so, too, do you imagine, or bring into the form of images, the very pathway that returns you to your true reality.

So, we now embark upon yet another lesson, another thirty-day period or so, in which *you* have the choice to become *fully committed* to heeding every word, to letting the vibration brought forth by that word to settle ever more deeply into your nervous system of the body, as it settles likewise, into the depth of your mind and your heart. Therefore, fear not, for you are the creator of your journey home. You are the creator of all that you perceive. You are the one given the Infinite Power of the Mind of God to see through the Eyes of Love, to rest in perfect safety, to embrace all that comes to you in the simple reality that you have called it to you—as a challenge, perhaps, but always as an opportunity to expand your *commitment* to Love. And where Love is chosen so that you want nothing else, beloved friends you will see nothing else but a lovely world, infinite in dimension, sparkling in clarity, radiant in beauty. And you will look upon it and say,

Behold, it is very good!

So! We would wish, then, in this hour, to begin to gently direct you toward something which will begin to be offered to you in the coming months. It will be offered, not through this monthly communication. It will not be offered through this, my beloved brother,

46

who continues in his commitment to offer himself to his Creator, to join with me by surrendering the possessiveness of the body-mind, and allows me to generate through him thoughts which are not his own. What will be offered in the coming months is a methodology for what you might call meditation. It will be refined somewhat, and changed to more perfectly meet your calling. But it is a form of communion, or meditation, that was initially and essentially taught by me to several of my friends, what you know as disciples, one of which carried this specific form of teaching and preserved it.

Now, it did not originate with me. I merely refined it. For I, like you, was once a student of the ways of seeking God. And I dove deep into the nature of consciousness and mind itself and discovered how to attune the mind, the emotions, and even the nervous system of the body to resonate with the Perfect Will and Love of God. Therefore, in your future months, this will indeed be coming forth through two who are humble of Spirit and pure of Heart, who have heard the call and have answered it. Whether or not you will take advantage of this will be up to you.

To begin to prepare a place for that teaching, we want to suggest for you that over the course of the next thirty days, and we speak here to many of you that you *return* to the practice of abiding as Christ for at least five minutes. Then, as that five-minute practice period is completed, allow the eyes to close. Become aware of the simple movement of your own breathing. And simply hold the thought,

I allow this breath to move more deeply and slowly.

Then, beginning to feel that sense of relaxation ever more deeply, hold the thought,

> *As Christ, in perfect safety, I release all tension. As Christ, in perfect safety, I dissolve my mind in the perfect Peace of God.*

Then, merely continue in this manner: as what you call the breath comes to fill the body gently, merely say,

> *I accept . . .*

and as the breath leaves the body, gently say within the mind,

> *. . . the Love of God.*

And again, as the breath enters the body,

> *I accept . . .*

and as it leaves the body,

> *. . . the Love of God.*

Continue in this manner for about five minutes—regardless of what the egoic mind says to you, and it will kick up a bit of a storm. Simply return to this simple practice.

At the end of about five minutes, let the prayer that you've been offering change from *words* to *energy.* You might perceive it as a golden white light; you might feel it as a gentle flow of relaxation—whatever works for you is fine. Continue gently to breathe that quality or that color, into yourself with each breath. And with each letting go of the breath, imagine and feel that energy moving throughout the course of the body, as though it were extending like a gentle breeze beyond the boundaries of the body.

And again, if the egoic consciousness kicks up its heels, and you start thinking of all the multitude of things you "ought" to be doing, simply return to the prayer. For all prayer is nothing more than a choice to abide, to contemplate, to rest in communion, beyond egoic thought. After about another five minutes, then say within the mind,

> *As Christ, I have celebrated in this manner the Truth of Who I Am. And I bring Peace to the world this day.*

Allow this practice period to occur in the morning of your day, and then again in the evening of your day. The only change would be in the final phrasing. Say simply,

> *This day I have brought Peace to the world and offered it to my companions.*

That should be clear enough for you and simple enough to begin. You may wish to use this taped message to play as a guide for you, for a period of time, until it seems more comfortable for you. Those that embark on this simple process will be well prepared for what is to come in the coming months. And now we'll continue with some other things.

Beloved friends, the world that you look upon is

not real! It has never been real. It will never be real. But it is a creation that can be *impregnated* with the Perfect Love of God. Remember always, then, that there is only Love or fear. And what is not Love can be *only* fear, and is never justified. The world that you have made is *thoroughly harmless.* The world that you experience, which is the world that you have made in conjunction with others, in any given moment offers to you the opportunity to choose to impregnate it with Love, or to allow it to reflect to you your fearful thoughts. You are not limited at any time, and in you all power under Heaven and Earth is given.

And you have a phrase in your world,

There is nothing to fear but fear itself.

That is ninety-eight percent accurate. Fear is the only energy that can separate you from the Kingdom. And fear is never justified in any moment. The final two percent would be to say there is nothing to fear, since fear is only a temporary insanity, and your right-mindedness is but a choice away. Therefore, begin to look upon each situation, each moment or minute of your life, as a very separate scene in a movie. It has its certain set, its certain characters. It has a beginning and it has an end. Because, although you are eternal, the things of time are not. And all things birthed in time, in time, will end in time.

Therefore, will you use the moment birthed in time to bring what is eternal to it? Or will you continue to believe that yet within you there is no possible power to choose Love over fear? Look around you. What do your eyes show you? Would you bless it or curse it? What would you teach yourself, and therefore make true for you?

Now, the message of this hour is being given slowly, deliberately, and carefully. For we want you to make no mistake in what is being shared—both in terms of practice and in theory. Theory is important in your world. For it is only through theory that the mind, the little part of you that is arrogant, will decide whether to value what the theory offers. And when you have placed value upon what the theory offers to you, you are then willing to embark on the practices it requires. I hope that makes sense to you.

Therefore in this hour, we are choosing to speak with you more rationally than emotionally. We would ask you to consider this: Have you suffered enough? Have you kept yourself small long enough? Have you tasted limitation deeply enough to know that you want these things no longer? Would you be willing to patiently choose the dissolving of your illusions? For on just the other side of each illusion is the freedom and peace that you seek.

And in any moment you can tell, quite clearly, what you are most committed to. If the body is tight and uncomfortable, if you must speak with a louder voice, if your words come more quickly, if the brow is furrowed and the jaw tense, rest assured you have chosen to be devoted to fear. You are like one who carries a magic wand filled with such power that you could merely wave it upon the face of this Earth and extend the Kingdom of Heaven to every heart and every mind. What, then, can prevent the expression of such power?—the fear that *you* have made to replace the reality of Love.

As you look upon each segment, each scene in your movie, each minute, begin to cultivate the deliberate practice of recognizing that where you are is in a field of energy which is your perfect servant. And within that moment, or that minute, *you* are the one with the power to make that moment be whatever you wish it to be. It can be filled with Christ Consciousness. It can be filled with temporary insanity. The choice is always yours. And never, ever, has there been such a thing as a victim.

Therefore, as you enter into any one of your minutes, ask of yourself,

> *What is this* for*? What do I decree this moment is to be? What do I most want to learn by teaching it?*

To teach is to *demonstrate.* To demonstrate is to *express* what you have decided will hold the greatest value for you. Whenever you judge another, you are decreeing that the thing of greatest value is separation, since judgment always causes contraction and, therefore, separation from another. When you practice forgiveness, you are decreeing that what you value is joining in holy and peace-filled relationship.

Remember that forgiveness has nothing at all to do with saying to another,

> *Well, I can see that you have sinned, but I forgive you your faults.*

No! Forgiveness is the recognition that *nothing* has

been done to you, that you would prefer to see the Face of Christ in the one in front of you. Let me give you an example on this marvelous Easter day. For it is not by accident that this hour's message has waited for this day.

Easter celebrates resurrection. It has been made to celebrate *my* resurrection. But this has only served to turn your attention from the *'specialness'* (and I say this in the sense of your *uniqueness*), the specialness of *your* existence, *your* reality, and placed your attention on mine and on me—as though Christ is something merely historical, that I am *'special'* in the Eyes of our God. Therefore, upon this Easter, recognize, then, that you have the power to celebrate and accept *your resurrection* as the Living Christ by seeing beyond the boundaries of death, and loss, and fear, and hurt, and anger, and projection, and the perceptions upon which projection rests. *You* are the one who has been reborn when you choose to remember only loving thoughts.

What, then, is the veil that seems to make it so difficult?

It can be only this: that you have accepted into your mind, at some level, that the world you see is real and that *it* holds *a power* to dictate to you whether you will feel peace or disturbance, Love or judgment. This is *always* an illusion. And your question on this Easter day is: Would you be willing to surrender your illusions in order to *re-member* the Perfect Peace of God?

The question on this, your Easter, is whether or

not you will accept the Atonement for yourself, the resurrection for yourself, and be determined to walk this Earth as one who has arisen. That is, you have chosen to awaken from the *uselessness* of separation, the uselessness of victimhood, the uselessness of weakness, to the *empowerment* of becoming responsible for this dimension of Creation, the empowerment of deciding to walk the Earth as the arisen Christ—to take the message of an historical event that did occur in time (for if it did not, somebody has managed to fool me), to take the message of an historical event and to assimilate it as a symbol of your own life. For you have well been crucified by your own thoughts. And by your own thoughts, you have brought your persecutors to you, who have nailed you on the cross a million times, so that you could be confronted with the opportunity to look out upon a lovely world by seeing only through the Eyes of Love.

Think, then, for a moment, and imagine that *you* are nailed upon a cross. You are stuck between the vertical axis of eternity and the horizontal axis of time and the body. Imagine that you lift your head, upon which *you* have placed a crown of thorns. And what does that represent? It represents the *field of the mind*, as it operates and expresses through the body, through the brain. Those thorns represent your fearful thoughts, your judgmental thoughts, your limited thoughts, that press and poke upon your own energy field and give you quite a cosmic headache, and draw blood. That is, it releases the Life force from you, the power from you, as it drains down your auric field. You dissipate yourself, much like a balloon with a slow leak dissipates the power that makes it a balloon.

'Crown of thorns' symbolizes the effect of the thoughts you insist upon when you rest in judgment, or anger, or hurt, or fear. That is, when you choose to deny Love. Now, the 'nails' merely represent that which would hold you stuck in a dimension, the horizontal dimension of the body and of time, that would nail your feet to the world. "Down to earth," they call it. And yet, above you, the crown of your head is open Heavenward. And you are free to receive the Love of God, to choose only loving thoughts, to look gently upon everyone and every event, seeing only perfect innocence.

And so imagine, now, that you lift your head and you realize,

> *The blood is dripping from my brow by my own hand. The crown of thorns was placed upon me by those who came to serve me, to shock me into the remembrance that I have allowed myself, at times, to have thoughts of negativity, limitation, and fear. No wonder I've had such a headache!*

You look to the left and to the right and you see your wrists bound to the horizontal plane by a nail, a hard piece of iron, cold and thoughtless. And how many times have you bound yourself to the things of time through your own thoughtlessness, your own coldness?

And now, you turn to look down at your feet, there, crossed over, resting gently upon a small wooden slab, with a nail through them, as though the world were saying,

Don't you dare try to rise above our level of consciousness. How dare you mirror to us the Truth of our being by always being so sickeningly loving.

The world will seek to nail you down to Earth by insisting that you think with it. For remember, always, that the *world* (we're not talking about the Earth, we are talking about the *world* of human experience) is the attempt to create that which is the opposite of Reality, like many who would gather together to take a drug and to think that their insanity is the same as the bliss and ecstasy of union with God. Yet they wouldn't dare drive an automobile, cannot think a coherent thought, and don't even remember where they are.

And now, you turn your eyes from the roar and the din of the world. You see the soldiers, your persecutors, totally unconscious, totally conformed to the authority of the world, so that they have donned the armor and the headpieces and the footwear and carry the spears of a god made as a substitute for Love. You look out upon the fearful crowd. You see some friends who still see your soul, your Christ Mindedness, and continue to love you. And yet even *they* are veiled by their belief that death and loss are possible. And so you are *completely alone.* No one is going to save you. No one is going to rescue you. It is between you and your God.

It is a decision, now, that you must make, to be determined to *choose only what is Real*, regardless of what the eyes seem to show you and what every mind around you seems to believe, even those who professed belief in your message of Love. For they look upon the body and an old belief takes hold,

> *The body is what is real after all. Look at this—it's nailed to a cross. This is limitation. This proves that the world's thinking is true.*

And so you must lift your eyes from the world that you think you see and choose to accept a different Reality:

> *Father, into Thy hands I commend my Spirit.*

Which is nothing more than the choice for *sanity* in the midst of all conditions, the choice for what is *eternal* in the field of what is temporal, the choice for what is *unlimited* in the field of what seems to be limitation, the choice for *sanity* in the field of what seems to be pervaded by insanity, the choice to *remember only thoughts born in Love!*

And then, your eyes look down again. And now something has changed—you are at peace. You recognize that you are above the world, you are above the crowd, and a *gentle sweetness* begins to pervade your entire beingness. All pain and suffering is forgotten. The nails can hold you no longer. And the world cannot keep you down in its insanity. The eyes of the body close, and as they close the world they had shown you recedes and the *real world* appears. And you rest in the perfect remembrance that you are One with God. And your attention drifts away from insanity. And yet, you are quite aware that you can still see your friends. You see the soldiers. You see the tears, the tumult. You see some who are merely standing quietly. And you bless them and release them to have the perceptions that they would choose. For you have come to love yourself so much that you will accept only what is Real.

It is finished.

The resurrection now begins.

Easter is your birthday. Easter is a time to celebrate that the crown of thorns has been removed because you have chosen to *think only loving thoughts*, that you have remembered the power given unto you through which you transcend the awful and dreaded and suffering-filled experience born of fear. For in Love there is only peace. And in Love there is only the infinitude of Pure Spirit. In Love is Christ restored to your consciousness. In Love are you returned.

Easter is for you and not for me. Therefore, set aside your images and your practices of me. Make no pilgrimage to me. Make a pilgrimage to the Heart of your *Self* by looking upon all that you see this day and seeing its beauty, its harmlessness, by knowing that *you* are looking out *through the eyes of the arisen Christ.* You are that One who, with me, has overcome the world. And what can there be left to do but to celebrate with your brothers and sisters? What can there be left to do but to laugh, to sing, to play, to remember, in quiet devotion, the Love your Creator has always had for you?

Here then, beloved friends, is the end of the message of this hour, this month, and even this day. You can choose *only* between Love and fear. In Love are you resurrected. In fear are you crucified. What, then, will be your choice in this hour in which death offers you Eternal Life? And with that, peace be unto you always.

We would ask that you listen to this message many times in your coming thirty days. For here alone do you find the magic doorway, set before you always. The only choice that matters is before you now, as it is always—Love or fear, resurrection or crucifixion, joy or suffering, unlimitedness or smallness. The choice is always yours. And like me, upon a cross so long ago, *no one can make the decision for you*. No one causes your perceptions. They flow from your choice for crucifixion or resurrection.

I know where *I* would choose to have you join me. Know, then, that I love you, often and always, in the ways that you will allow and to the depth that you will accept. Choose, then, with me and we are free. Peace, beloved friends, peace to the Only Begotten of God . . . the Resurrected Christ, or the crucified body and egoic mind?

Amen

Lesson Four

Now, we begin.

And once again, greetings unto you, beloved and holy friends. As always, it is a joy to come forth and abide with you in this manner. And we have come forth this day to communicate through this, our beloved brother, as we continue with you in *The Way of Transformation*.

Within the word, itself, there is great wisdom. *Transformation* requires that there be that which abides *in form*. And you are that. You are Spirit. You are that which has come forth as a ray of Light from the Mind of God, as a sunbeam to the sun. And in that form-less beginning, you are Consciousness, Itself. You are Intelligence, Itself. You are bliss; you are radiance; you are compassion. You are the potential for endless creativity.

You *are* God Itself. Now, that is the first time that we've been quite so bold—as we have sought gently over the years, for many of you that have been around that long, have been willing to stay the course—it is the first time that we have described *you* as Spirit, as That which *is* God. This can only mean that what you are in your essence, in your essential being, *is* God Himself.

The very first level of Creation, then, is when That which we call God, or Abba, first began the indescribable, the unexplainable mystery of birthing Himself forth, out of the eternal matrix of his Being. That first level of Creation was Pure Spirit—a *subtle, subtle movement* in which a gentle

Sunbeam begins to emerge from the Sun, or a ray of Light soundlessly begins to emanate from Light Itself. In Pure Spirit, you *are* unbounded; you are without form. But you are *not* without Consciousness. You're not without Self-awareness. In Spirit, there is only Self—not self and other, not self apart from form, but simply Self . . . radiant, shimmering, unbounded, alone, yet not lonely. Rather, filled with Self, filled with God, filled with Love.

This first level of Creation *never changes*. It is as God, Itself.

For the Sunbeam is as the Sun; the ray of Light as the Light. A momentum, though, has begun—a momentum extending from the Pure Potentiality of All That God Is. For Love seeks only to *extend* Itself. Extension is an activity, it is a movement. And for there to be extension, there must necessarily have then been created what you *call* space. But even at this level of Creation, the space of which we speak is not quite what you would perceive in your mind, as you think of that which contains the planets whirling around your sun.

Rather, it was more like a, let us say, a mathematical concept. It was the *idea* of space, in which extension could occur. There were not yet planets and suns. There was not yet a single atom or molecule of what you call matter. There was Pure Thought, Pure Love, Pure Being, beginning to *entertain* (and I emphasize that word for a certain reason), to *entertain* the idea of pure space, pure extension—unlimited, unbounded, forever. There was Pure Spirit. *That is what You Are*, now and forever. *Spirit does not change.*

There is, then, that which in you, right here and right now, even as you listen to these words, even as you perceive yourself as a body sitting in a chair or lying on the floor (preferably not driving an automobile)—right here and right now, beyond all that you see with your physical eyes, all that you are aware as and within the body, beyond the activity of the surface level of the mind which you are most familiar with, in which there is what is called the firing of the neurons in the brain, almost without ceasing, so that the mind seems to never be without images and thoughts ... far beyond this planet, and yet right where this planet abides, far beyond this universe, and yet right where this universe abides, far beyond all dimensions, the infinite dimensions of Creation, yet right where those infinite dimensions exist: *Spirit Is.*

Here is found what I have often referred to as the "real world." Here, peace abides *eternally* with perfect consistency and without interruption. Here, *the Living Reality is,* which has been reflected in the sentence,

I and My Father are One.

In other words, when Consciousness transcends Its perception of Itself as being only conditional existence—being only the *forms* of existence (the body-mind, the particular sense of self as separate from all other selves, the blade of grass, the cloud in the sky, the rock upon the ground)—when Consciousness transcends this sense of Itself, It abides not in a thinking relationship. It doesn't observe Spirit as something else and then say,

Oh, that's what I am. Great.

Rather, there is a living sense in which Consciousness as such, as the Self, rests in the Self and simply *knows*. For only knowledge is *immediate*, and not mediated by any concept, form, or experience.

In such a moment, and it takes only a moment, there is immediate awakening to the Reality of the real world. And in some form, then—and notice I said in some *form*—as Consciousness then dances back into the *extension* of Spirit, into the *extension* of Reality, into creativity, into Creation—in the *human* form it can say,

I and My Father are One.

There are many such statements within the human family that have been uttered to express that awakening, that Reality.

Now, in this ceaseless movement from That which never moves, as the ray of Light emerges from Light Divine—unbounded, eternal, unobstructed—in the very desire to be creative, to extend creativity ceaselessly (and that is what Creation is), Spirit begins to *condense* or *descend* (these are both very spatial terms). And, again, we are now using language that finds its source on your side of the fence; that is, on the side of the fence of phenomenal existence, not on the side of the fence of Spirit, where language is hardly required. Spirit continues its dance, as the One Mind, God the Father, *entertains* the extension of Creation. And Spirit begins to *condense* into something that has not yet ever occurred. The thought, and again, we are still operating at a level of Pure Thought, Pure Potentiality—there is not yet the deep darkness of the space of your universe or of any dimension whatsoever—it begins to condense into a thought of *individuation*.

You have all seen, perhaps, in your commercials on your televisions, when the milk is poured into the glass in slow motion. And as the milk hits the glass it begins to move back up the sides, as the cup begins to fill. And at the last moment, when the carton is tilted back and the pouring has stopped, the motion that has been started creates the phenomenon of a circular drop of milk which arises and, for a very temporary moment, seems to become separated from the body of milk in the glass, itself. It emerges and in a split second, you who are watching the screen, have the *awareness* of an individuated drop of milk that seems to exist completely independent of the body of milk, itself. And then in the next moment it drops back into the body of milk itself, and you *lose awareness* of it as a separate thing, a separate drop of milk. But it was still milk. From your place of perception, it merely looked *as though* it had separate existence.

Now, that is an analogy, of course, since the Soul is not made of milk. But it does create a picture for you of what occurs when the body of Spirit continues in its entertainment of creativity, out of which that which emerges, which we have called Soul—the *first, subtle inception* of the thought of *individuation*, of that which is an individuated expression of the fullness of Spirit, which is Light, which is God.

And why? All for the joy of extending Creation, that That One might be aware of Itself in an endless variety of form. And this is where it begins—the *delight* of Creation. That is what You Are! In Pure Soul there is still only Pure Potentiality. There has not yet been what you would know as experience. There is, however, the first subtle awareness of the One Self being aware of Itself.

As Soul continues the extension of Light, of Pure Creativity, it condenses. It descends to the next level, if you will. And, again, since we're using language from your side of the fence, there are not many other ways to speak of this. The Soul descends or condenses, and begins to create a deeper awareness of Itself as an individuated *thing*.

Now, Its awareness of Itself as Spirit is taking on a new coloration, a new vibration. It is becoming very close to what many of you have experienced in your own meditations and prayer, or the time you heard a child cry, or you walked through a forest at dawn—when your egoic mind was temporarily transcended, and you had a sense of your Oneness with God, and yet still felt other than God—creature and Creator, Son and Father—united, yet *somehow* different.

Here is where the separation can be said to have occurred. For it is *here*, in the first level of Pure Potentiality of this unique thought, that That which Intelligence Is, That which Love Is, That which Light Is (and I have referred to this, for instance, in *A Course in Miracles*, as Mind. And Mind is not merely the prattling that goes on in the human brain, that you refer to as "thinking." Mind is much more vast than that!)—it is here in the first level of subtle perception of the Self as an individuated matrix of awareness, that has awareness of Itself, and yet that Self, or God, is somehow something different than what the Soul perceives to be Itself . . . *here* is where the first, unique thought of separation is birthed, at this very *subtle* point . . . long before the planets of your universe arose, long before the multidimensionality of Creation came into being. Here, you are. Here, there is but One Soul, a unique expression of the One Spirit, Itself the unique expression of That One who eternally Is.

Here, creativity gives rise to the power of thought. And it is from the Field of Thought, Pure Thought, that Creation will now begin to spring immediately into being. And here, at this subtle level, the drop of milk has seemingly separated Itself and now *feels awareness* of Itself as separate from the body of milk. And for a moment, for just a moment, there is pure joy, because it's still the One doing it—out of entertainment, out of pure play, out of the sheer exuberance of extending Itself and Its infinite Power, ceaselessly and without limitation. For you see, if God, Who becomes you, held the thought,

Well, I certainly can't separate My Self from My Self,

that would be a limitation.

And so, the One creates a drop of Itself, along with the *perception* that It perceives Itself as separate, from something which is now, for the first time, *other*. Here is the germination, the seed planted, for egoic consciousness. But that's still a little further along in the story.

As that first thought of separation is dreamt, a new energy is born. That which has been pure joy, that which has been pure freedom, pure safety, now changes form slightly. You could say a drop of milk within the drop of milk seems to separate and take on its own energy. And that we have called *fear*. Here is born not extension, but *contraction*, or the *experience* of contraction, as fear emerges in awareness. And now the river begins to cascade very, very quickly—out of fear, out of the first inception of the thought,

> *I am alone. I am separate from my Creator.*

And yet, remember, in reality, it's the Creator perceiving the Creator, and creating the perception that God is separate from God.

With that thought, an explosion occurs—very like what your scientists have called the "Big Bang." They don't know how close they are! They merely need to make the shift to seeing that the Big Bang occurred in *Consciousness, Itself*, not out of pure *matter*, whatever that was. In the Big Bang of Consciousness, suddenly imagine that drop of milk exploding in *space*, which comes into being with the thought of separation, and becoming an infinite array, or number of points—little droplets of milk, little droplets of Consciousness, little sparks of Divinity, little particles of Light.

To use yet another analogy from your realm of science, the wave of light has now become the *particles of light*. When and why, who can say? Only

that One, who is doing the birthing of Itself, knows.
And *you are That One.*

As these particles of light are now *spread* (and, again,
we have another spatial term), *spread out* through
the infinite reaches of the Pure Potentiality of
Spirit—which is Light, which is God—each particle
possesses the exact same potential. In fact, you could
not, shall we say, find any difference between the
points of Light, whatsoever—*none.* If you were to
measure them, they'd be the same size, although
they have no size. If you measured their frequency
or vibration, they'd all be the same—identical points
of Light that *seem to* have now taken existence in
different points of space.

That is, there is the sense that while they are identical
in quality and substance, there is a slight difference in
the space that each one occupies, as though you took
two identical pencils and put one on the left side of
the table, and one on the right. Still made of the same
substance, but now, in the vast continuum of space,
that which is identical is occupying two points of
space, each with the perfect freedom mirroring the
perfect freedom of the one God . . . infinite rays of
Light, now mirroring and reflecting the perfection of
the freedom of Pure Potentiality, which is the Light
Itself—*the Pure Potentiality to create.* Each one has
within it the thought, the recognition, the perception,
that is, of separation. Fear has been birthed:

> *I am alone. I am not that point of Light over there. I
> am just myself.*

And as the energy of fear continues, the contraction,

the condensation, the descension continues. And now, what has burst forth, again, instantaneously (this is not yet requiring time), is the *multitude*, the infinite multidimensionality which is Creation, except for one thing: the physical universe has not yet been birthed. The physical universe *requires* the concept of *time*. For only in time does the physical dimension exist.

And so, here is where you begin to discover what has been called in your language, from your side of the fence, the hierarchy of angelic beings, of angelic worlds. Just points of Light, just like you, but not in the experience of time, nor in the condensation that you would call physical bodies—not even the lower astral bodies. Still, multidimensionality of creativity is a radiant dance with just a tinge of a sense of separation, or "otherness," or fear.

In this multidimensionality, which is still pervaded and is as Light Itself, condensation continues. And here your scientists begin to tap into it, so you can see how many steps removed they are! But here Light begins to condense into the particles of matter. And again, the explosion occurs, as the one, you could say the one basic atom—or *Adam,* hmm—explodes in the Big Bang. And the multitude of bodies, of planetary bodies, including your central sun of your tiny little universe, is birthed.

And the physical universe, of which you know that you are a part as a human being, is vast beyond comprehension. And yet, it is as a tiny speck of dust. It is as a tiny speck of Light, floating seemingly freely—like a tiny drop of milk that seems to have separated itself from the body of milk—your physical universe seems to float freely and is unaware of the multidimensionality of radiant Light and Spirit and God *in which it floats*, out of which it has been given its very *existence*. You are, therefore, not outside of Spirit. You could say you are held lovingly—your whole physical dimension—in the *center* of Spirit.

As this condensation continues, what you call, or have been told to call *"life"* begins. Conditions are set up, emerging from what—pure chance?—hardly . . . but out of the Pure Potentiality, the Power and the Perfect Intelligence *to create*—though now that creativity is expressing itself, more and more, out of fear, not out of pure joy. It's like taking a note of a flute and muffling it slightly, so that it has a different quality. Yet pure energy it still is. For what can fear be but energy? . . . as Love is energy, as compassion is energy, as sadness is energy, as anger is energy.

Do you see? Fear is just an energy, and nothing more. In itself, it is *perfectly neutral*. For *all events are neutral*. And fear, being merely a dance or a play of energy itself, must be an entirely neutral event, until something arises to perceive and experience it differently. And what is that? To make a story which is not quite conducive to our needs, we'll skip that and simply come to this: the birth of egoic consciousness.

And here *fear* has *condensed* into its *final form*. There can be no further condensation of the energy which has become fear, for egoic consciousness *is fear-full consciousness* . . . *The ego is fear*. And yet, it is made of Pure Power, Pure Potentiality, Unlimited Creativity. And rest assured, you all have the experience of knowing just how ceaselessly creative egoic mind can be. For without ceasing, it knows how to immediately look upon another brother or sister, upon an event upon the planet, it can look upon anything, and that fast, in the twinkling of an eye, in a space that doesn't even require a thought, egoic consciousness can change its values, can change its perceptions, to create what it wants to create. And what it wants to create is that which continues its existence.

Much like in your physical body, when a cell becomes cancerous and decides to run amok, and act as though it were not dependent on the laws of the body itself, that keep the body healthy, it begins to do what? It begins to create cells like unto itself. Cancer is merely a misperception run amok at the level of the body—thinking for *itself*, creating in *its own image* rather than *extending* the image, if you will, of the Creator; living out of harmony with the One Mind that creates in radiant joy for no other reason than to extend the good, the holy, and the beautiful. And yet, God does not create limitation, does not withdraw creativity from the power of the ego. Rather, because God is Love, all power under Heaven and Earth is available and can be tapped into by egoic consciousness.

So what is egoic consciousness? You all know what it feels to be *absolutely certain* that you are separate and alone, that you must rely on your own thinking process, and that no one beyond—not just the boundary of your body or skin—but no one beyond your unique, contracted sense of "I" has any connection to you whatsoever, and no one cares:

> *I am alone. I am separate. How on earth am I going to make it? I've got to figure my own way. I've got to figure out how this world works. I've got to make it happen for myself!*

Fear has taken its final form. Now, there is a complete forgetting of God, of the One, of Spirit, *even of Soul.* The body represents a level of vibration, still quite intelligent, still *very* intelligent. It is like a matrix of energy, the very thought of condensation into human form, out of which forms keep getting created, keep getting created, keep getting created, keep getting created. And you've done that for yourself an infinite number of times.

The *body* is the *representation of the ego.* For notice that as you sit in your chair, you are quite certain you're not the wall across from you. As you sit where you are in your chair, your consciousness, your awareness, seems to tell you that you are the listener and not the speaker, that it wasn't you that sat into a chair and had Jeshua ben Joseph, and a certain lineage or vibration of consciousness, radiate thought down through the mind–body matrix that used to be exclusively owned by someone named Jon Marc. Hmm. *You* are not that one:

> *No, no, not me. I couldn't do that if I wanted to. That must make Jon Marc special. And* certainly *it makes Jeshua* very *special! For I am just this blob of dust, this separate mind-body, sitting in my chair, on the floor, or a couch, listening to a tape filled with words which vibrate with a certain meaning, and create certain pictures and understandings in my mind. But these are being placed within me, and I*

am not that one.

That is egoic consciousness:

> *I am* not *That One. I am* not *God. I am* not *pure Spirit. I am* not *Pure Soul. I am this thing that sits in this chair, now.*

And do you know something? You're absolutely right—you *are* that! That and so much more!

So the egoic mind is that which creates the separated perception that it is only one tiny thin slice of the pie. It creates a delusion, a distortion, in Consciousness Itself, like a little blip on one of the radar screens—that creates just a little blip, that tells the one watching the screen that there is some *thing* there.

> *I am separate. I am alone. I cannot think with the Mind of God. I cannot experience Unity Consciousness. I cannot be as Jeshua is. No, not me. I, I'm too small and too weak. Oh, I just don't have it together yet. Maybe someday . . .*

Yet all the while, *you are that One.* And by the Power of that One, you have the potential to think the thought,

> *I could never be like Jeshua is. I'm really too small, and too fragile, and too weak, and too stupid. Oh, the Christ Consciousness may be there for someone else, but not for me.*

The whole while, *that very thought* must *use* the Power of the One. For that Power is Life! That Power is Pure Being! That Power is the real world! That Power is the only thing that exists—*period!* By the Power of that One, you have dreamt the thought of the separate self. By the Power of that One, when you decide to, you will awaken from the thought of egoic consciousness.

Now, why is all of this important? For beloved friends, *The Way of Transformation* requires that there be that which exists *in form. You* exist in form. You're sitting in a chair. You know the space and volume of a human body. You know the particular thoughts which you identify as your own. You have a history to that body-mind that emerged—well, let's face it, as you experience the body-mind, it emerged from sexual desire between two beings called parents who got together. And a little thing wiggled its way up to touch another thing, and there was a burst of Light, and a pure spark of Pure Soul made a *decision* from *intentionality* to become fixated or identified with, and as, a physical form.

So, having a good time on a Saturday night is the source of your being—as a bodily being. And that's, of course, if you were lucky, where both parents consciously desired to use the body as a communication device for teaching only Love; and gave one unto another, and then accepted that little spark of Light that begins yet the birthing of another body, and clearly invited another Soul to come and abide with them, as teacher and friend, as brother or sister. Unfortunately, that is yet rare upon your planet.

That is the matrix into which you have descended, time and time again, as you have come to teach yourself that you are just a separate, lonely, failing, weak individual. At the death of the body you have found yourself as Soul, and been frightened by the radiance of your Light, because that Light is not the same as your interpretation that you had learned of yourself. Fear causes condensation, contraction, *falling* if you will. And what you fall into is a matrix of energy that best resonates with *your own* perception and belief about yourself. Belief is not just thought. It is *a quality of vibration*. And you fall, yet again, into a field of energy, into a dream, into a physical universe, into a time frame, into a family structure that resonates and vibrates with how you have learned to perceive yourself.

And all the while you are yet That One: radiant, perfectly free, using the very Power of God to create and believe in a dream of smallness, weakness, separation, loneliness. Right now, as you listen to these very words, *now*, that's what you're doing. You are choosing how you will think of yourself. And how you think of yourself is reflected in the world that you see, in the experiences that are manifest within your own particular universe of consciousness.

If you knew that you were the Unlimited One, you would never fear the creation of the golden coins again. You would never believe that you must live in lack. But you are still, for the most part, clinging to the belief that you are that small little thought of separation called egoic mind, still struggling to find God, not recognizing that it is the very Power of God's presence from which you create the perception you hold of yourself.

So, there you are—sitting upon your chair, lying upon your floor, sitting upon your couch. And you are That One. You are *in form*, that is, you have created a perception of your self that includes the experience of being a body-mind, which, by the way, *is* separate from all other bodies. It *is* separate from the rock. Obviously, you can look out your window and tell that where the body is that you identify with, is in a different spatial point than every other object. That's what this world is! This universe is the *attempt* to create a reflection that *convinces* you that the first fearful thought of separation *is* the *truth* of who you *are*! You are using, or have unwittingly been using, your physical universe to constantly reflect to you what *must be* the *truth*: that *you are separate from all Creation.*

This world is nothing but the reflection of *that thought*. And yet, even here, That One pervades all things, and the realization of your Self *as* That One is closer to you than your own breath—simply a decision away. Here, there is great richness not found in any other dimension, the richness of the *dramas* of separation, of seeking—seeking, seeking, seeking.

> *Well, I have read the* Course in Miracles *one time, and it didn't seem to work—I'll read it again. Oh, that didn't work. Well, maybe I'll go try this form of meditation. No, that didn't work. Maybe I'll try Buddhism. No, that didn't work. I'll try Christianity. No, that didn't work. I'll try drugs—that will do it!*

The very energy of seeking *is* the egoic energy. For only the ego can *seek*. Pure Spirit can only *extend*. And there is a huge difference!

Egoic consciousness, as you well know, plays itself out through the forms of *special relationships*. You have a special relationship with your employer; you have a special relationship with your spouse, your lovers, your car, your boats, your automobiles. And the world plays off of your need for specialness.

> *Oh, look at this automobile. Mmm . . . isn't this one sexy?! Oh, you're going to feel so-o-o good!*

So, you seek to create the means to possess that certain automobile.

> *Oh, if only I had that person as my spouse. Oh, let me seek that one by seducing that one. I'll act as though I'm other than my poor, paltry, lonely self, so that they think I am grand. I will ruffle up my peacock feathers.*

Hmm . . . interesting that we would use the word "pea-cock" to demonstrate the flowering forth of the great feathers that seduces the mate to come!

And on it goes. The world is the reflection of the belief in the *need* for special relationship. And the search for that is the restlessness that you feel—that restlessness that you feel in the mind, that creates the waves of restlessness in the fluids and subtle energies, which are contained within and make up the illusion of the body. The restlessness of the breath, the tightness of the muscles, the loneliness as you rest your head upon the pillow at night, for you believe that you are that body-mind, separate and alone, apart from all others.

And the infinite, eternal stream of communication that occurs throughout Creation, unobstructedly, is lost to your awareness. And yet, so close are you. It requires only a thought to shift the momentum in a new direction, to rest your head upon the pillow and say,

> *I am not just this body-mind. I am That One, pure, unbounded and undefiled. I am in communication with every rock and every tree and every time frame that has ever been.*

And, yes, when you begin that thought, it will seem wholly insane, because you've been on the other side of the fence, looking at Reality from a certain perspective. It fits like a glove upon the hand, but that does not make it right or true. Insanity seems sane to those who are insane. So that's just the way it is.

But the end of all seeking occurs when one *dares* to hold within the mind a *different* thought. And you have heard it many times through this, my beloved brother, through many of my other channels, through *A Course in Miracles*:

Only Love is Real.

You are not the body.

I and my Father are One.

I am awake and walk this planet as Christ.

I choose Love over fear.

What does that mean? Love is Pure Spirit. Fear is contraction, density, false perception—egoic consciousness. When you choose Love over fear, you must *decide* not to respond according to the momentum of egoic consciousness. You must decide to live as though you are not the ego. And in this way, what has been *formed* becomes *transformed*—that which pervades and extends beyond what has been formed: *transformed*.

The Way of Transformation, then, requires that you begin with the acceptance of what is true always. And in this hour, we have sought to bring to you a story, an analogy, a description that can help, if you will sit with it, to imprint into your consciousness a remembrance of the very process that you have, in fact, felt and experienced *as God, Itself,* in *Its* desire to create, in *His* desire to create, in *Her* desire to create—put it any way you wish—the One becomes what you perceive as the many, yet remains always the One.

And that is what you are! You are the song of the bird. You are the radiance and warmth of the sun as it touches the skin. You are the skin. You are the awareness of that warmth. You are the thinker of the thought. You are the thought. You are the deed. You are the space from which all thought emerges. You are the wind in the trees. You are the vastness of space. You are That One who is eternal. You are the one bold enough to dream the dream of separation, without ever losing perfect unity. And you are the One, the little drop of milk, experiencing the remembrance of the Divine, of the Real, of the True, of the One.

Your journey is not alone. And even now, you are perfectly awake. For only one who is awake could *dare* to create the great cleverness, and creativity, through which you, as a spark of God, become increasingly aware of your Self: *God diving into God; God discovering God!* What a delightful, delightful play!

And here, then, we begin to let the secret out of the bag. Separation was not because you sinned. Separation was not because something *terrible* went wrong. Separation was just another form of the Dance of Creation Itself—perhaps taken to the extremes, for God seeks the limits of what is unlimited.

You've been playing a game of Hide and Seek. You are the One with your eyes closed, leaning against the trunk of a tree, counting, while the fragments of your Self ran to hide. And you are the One who has reached out to discover those fragments, and is in the process of doing that. You are the One who has become the many, and then has waited to be discovered by that One. You are the Soul waiting to be touched by Grace. You are the separate One hiding in the darkness, trembling, and yet wanting Light to find you.

Why not begin now, in this moment, by sitting quietly as Christ, for five minutes? And say to the One who is coming, now, from the trunk of the tree:

> *I've done a very good job of hiding. But you know, I think it would be a great delight to be found! Find me, dear Father. Touch me with Your Grace. And because I*

am You, I will decide to receive it. And in that moment, I choose now to remember that I am the One who has both sought and found. I am the One who has remained perfectly unchanging forever. And I am the One who has perceived my Self as having changed, as having sinned, as having separated my Self.

I choose, now, to join the two parts of my Self together. And I will be a body-mind upon this planet—dancing, and singing, and playing, and creating the good, the holy, and the beautiful. And I will now open that part of my mind that can think in unlimited ways, that will dare to dream the impossible dream. I am that One who lets God live in me now! I and my Father are One! I am the drop of milk again settling into the fullness of the glass in which my Father dwells as milk.

And when I walk with this body upon this Earth, and I feel the mist of the fog upon my skin, I will say within myself, "Ah, yes, it is very good!" For I am that One with the power to create this body, to create the mist of the fog, itself. And the fog and the mist around me is as my Father's Presence in which my Soul reclines.

This world—no longer a burden. This world of space and time—no longer something from which I must escape. Not even sickness and dis-ease is a limitation for me. For wherever I am, I Am the presence of Love. And this moment, I bring forth Love and bless the world I see.

And in this, *God remembers God.* For beloved friends, *The Way of Transformation* must bring you, in the end, to the quiet recognition: *There is only God.* Why fear, if Love is here? And there is only Love or fear.

Peace, then, be unto you, beloved and holy friends. "Friends" because you are a part of me, and I a part of you—particles of Light dancing in the wave of the One God, the One Mind, the One Truth, the Real World. The joke has been on us! And we played it upon ourselves well. And now the time of rejoicing is at hand, as we arise in our individuation, recognizing our Oneness—to dance the Dance of Creation ceaselessly, extending only the *good*, the *holy*, and the *beautiful*.

Peace be unto the Only Begotten of God . . . God's Own.

GOD IS! Amen.

Lesson Five

Now, we begin.

And again, greetings unto you, beloved and holy friends. We come forth in this hour to continue our discussion of *The Way of Transformation*. We come forth in this hour to yet again remind you that all that you think, all that you see, and all that you do is not the result of that which comes *to* you, but rather, that which comes *from* you. For always and forever, the world you perceive is uncaused, save by yourself. This is why it is always true that freedom *is* closer to you than your own breath. That freedom *is* the reality of your being. That freedom *is* that which is realized without effort. Freedom is realized when you decide to accept the Truth that is true always:

I and my Father are One.

I Am That Which I Am.

You are Consciousness. You are Awareness. You are that which witnesses, that which experiences, that which pays homage to the one thing that God has created: *Christ.* Christ, then, means "the anointed." You have been anointed since before the beginning of all worlds with that which the Father Is: Awareness, Pure Intelligence. You have been anointed with the ability to choose what you would wish to perceive. And thereby imbued with the power to create, you abide—freely—in each moment.

This freedom is completely unobstructed and unchangeable, forever. It is in your freedom that you think what you think, you see what you see, you feel what you feel—even in your third-dimensional reality. At any moment, you are perfectly free to see the radiant beauty of the real world pervading all things, even your own consciousness, just as you are also free to see fear.

In our last hour together we began to explore, by way of analogy, that which has transpired that brought you into the experience of being a spark of the Divine, an aspect of the totality that brought you to the place of the soul. And the soul then condenses, falls if you will, into what you have called your physical world. And there you find yourself, right here and right now, surely the product of the world around you, surely the product of your parents, surely the product of forces beyond your control. And yet, the whole while, you have remained exactly as you are—the witness, pure consciousness, the Self, the seer, as some have called it.

Beloved friends, from the moment . . . now we are going to speak in this hour specifically about *this one life* that you're living now. Beloved friends, in the moment prior to your incarnation, you were in existence, abiding with perfectly clear awareness within a state or quality or dimension of consciousness. Now, it is true that even that was the result of choices made in the past. But again, we wish to speak in this hour of this one incarnation. Now, imagine then, if you will . . . perhaps you might wish to pause the tape, allow the body to relax. Let go of any gripping in the mind. Let the things that need perhaps to be done to, shall we say, sit on the shelf for awhile, and then continue.

Beloved friend, imagine, if you will, abiding without a physical body and yet having awareness. This should not be difficult, since you do it each night while you sleep. You do it when you "daydream." It occurs occasionally while making love, while watching your television. In fact, each and every one of you experiences that quality of awareness several times during each and every day, when you "forget yourself"—that is, you forget your *embodied existence*. The difference being that in your world, you "come back to your senses"—that is, you come back to embodied existence.

Imagine, though, a state in which there simply is no physical form, and you are abiding as Consciousness, Itself. Oh yes, you have awareness. Oh yes, you have form, but that form of energy has not condensed into the third dimension. You have friends. That is, you have other consciousnesses with which you are in perfect communication. For the vast majority of you, in fact we would say here in this hour, all of you that are listening to this tape as it is first given out, all of you are sufficiently evolved to have come into this life of yours, now, from a state of consciousness that is quite peaceful, quite joyous. Communication with those which we would call as *"friends"* is unbroken. It is consistent; it is respectful; it is loving; it is free.

As you relax and listen to this simple description, what color, or colors, begin to come to mind? Notice them, pay attention to them. What images seem to fleetingly flow through the mind? Notice them. Pay a moment's attention to them. For remember an ancient truth we once gave you: You cannot imagine that which you have not experienced, for imagination is the picturing in the conscious mind. That picturing must come forth from something. Mind, as you know it, can only picture what is or has been. It can then, of course, find ways, at times, to bring it back in to the third-dimensional experience, but that does not mean that it is new.

As you were abiding in that state, you were in relationship. Most of you were multidimensionally aware, that is, while you had a predominant color or level of energy, you were aware that you were surrounded at all times by other dimensions. Many of you communicated multidimensionally, both with that which would be called of a higher frequency as well as with that which would be called of a lower frequency. Many of you communicated with beings who were incarnated within the third-dimensional realm.

Now, there was a moment, for each and every one of you, when the decision was made within *your* consciousness, within *your* mind, that conditions were appropriate for you to again incarnate. There are many, many factors that attract the soul to yet again condense into physical form, but the chief among these is the perception and thought that there is yet something left undone, there is yet some lesson that cannot be realized save within the physical domain, that there is indeed a purpose that you, as a soul, would yet wish to fulfill.

It is very true that some of you have incarnated because you felt compassion. That is, you looked upon the third-dimensional realm and saw it suffering and *yearned* to bring Light to this dimension, in which you now find yourself. And yet even *this* stems forth from the reason, or the perception, that *you* must *do something* to *correct* what is occurring. That is a perception that many of you are aware still runs you. As you look out upon the world, as you look out upon your brothers and sisters, there is this *compulsion*, this need to get involved, to *fix*. There is a belief in many of you that if you take no action, that somehow *you* are belittled, that your sense of identity, your sense of being, is caught up with looking out upon the world, judging what is right and wrong, holding opinions about what *ought* to be done, and then often trying to persuade others to do it your way.

So, there you are. You are Spirit, and yet you are soul. You are having a relational experience and you are perfectly aware. Time does not quite exist where you are, for time is a unique and peculiar experience that is very much linked to matter or to the body. You abide in a timeless state. As you look upon the conditions, you are also aware of your connection with souls that you've known before, that are currently incarnated upon the physical plane. You are aware of, you can sense, the quality of a resonance of their consciousness with yours, that is, with the lessons you are longing to learn. A decision is made in the mind, *not forced upon you, whatsoever*. In fact, we would share with you that the decision to incarnate need not have *ever* been made. That is, you are not compelled by some force outside of yourself to come into this dimension. Does that mean that you made a mistake? Not at all. There can be no mistakes in all of Creation.

As you begin to *descend*, which means to bring your attention to slow its vibration of consciousness down, as you begin to *incarnate*, you did not so much *go* anywhere as merely—shall we say—turn your thermostat down, so that the quality of your consciousness, your essence, your soul, began to vibrate at a frequency that resonated with the third-dimensional plane. Your attention, your focus, your desire, began more and more to be focused on one unique, particular set of circumstances. These circumstances are *the web of relationship* created by the parents, created by the cultural milieu in which they live, the quality of consciousness—that field of energy, if you will, like a spinning vortex, itself a spinning vortex within a larger spinning vortex called the world, itself. And from your place of perception, the world is not solid at all. It's just another dimension of vibration, and that is all, with its own peculiar parameters.

And so you as soul, you as individuated consciousness, began to descend into incarnation. This cannot occur before the moment of conception in your mother's womb. Usually it is at that point of conception when you, as a soul, become involved in the very act by which conception occurs. And a new form of life begins to develop within the womb. In that moment, there is a flash, what you might call a quantum leap, and your attention becomes almost entirely fixated on, identified with, the particular quality of energy that is that new birthing of a physical form. You've "come into body," as they say it. Coming into body simply means that you've fixated your attention away from all other dimensions and have "taken on," if you will, the unique and particular and, sometimes, very peculiar parameters involved in that physical form. And what is that physical form made of? Inert matter?—hardly. It is, itself, a web of relationships created by the particular vibrational patterns of the mother and the father.

Therefore, as you come into this world, the very first relationships that you have are with the mother and father, and you know and feel them intimately. For you are now identified with a growing physical form that is, itself, growing out of—like a wave coming out of a particular ocean—it is growing *out of* the matrix of energies that make up the mother and the father.

Here is also where your "struggle" begins, your struggle to create yourself in the world. Your struggle begins to find yourself. For the majority of you, this process whereby attention is shifted from a different state of consciousness into the physical dimension . . . for the majority of you, this flash, this quantum leap, this shifting of attention, was so dramatic and required such a *shock* that you began to forget your connection to Spirit, your realization that you are soul, Pure Consciousness. You began to lose awareness of your freedom. You could call it *becoming unconscious*, or *falling asleep*.

Now, the very first universe that you experience within the physical dimension is the experience, or the universe, of the womb. Here, you are in *constant, constant* communication with all that is passing through the energy field of the mother. This doesn't mean just the potpie she had for dinner, or the cup of coffee she had in the morning which made your heart race (hmm?). It is also the quality of air that she breathes. But more important than these, the quality of *emotional energy* that makes up the particular matrix she is experiencing in her own universe. For these things immediately affect the hormonal balances, the flow of chemicals through the physiological system and, at this point, you are very much part of that physiological system. Therefore, you take on, you begin to *feel* and *experience* the psychic field of the mother. You are also aware of the psychic field of the father and of any other immediate family members. You are also aware of the energies, any particular dominant energies that are going on within the social structure. Remember we talked before about *webs of relationship*. You are a field of energy within a field of energy within a field of energy within a field of energy, even in your third-dimensional realm.

Many have used the word *imprint* to describe this initial state in which you become identified with the physiological form emerging out of the field of energy that is the particular matrix of the mixture of energies of the mother and father. This is where you start. And again, you have done so in order to bring forth what you would call certain lessons. You have done this because of certain patterns held within the consciousness before you turned your attention to this dimension. And again, for the vast majority of you, in fact all of you listening to this tape, that descension, that quantum leap from the realm of Pure Spirit from a different vibrational state, into the vibrational state of the third dimension, was a *shock*—so much so that your awareness *forgot yourself* as Pure Spirit.

Now, if the shock at conception isn't sufficient, it could happen any time during the womb. If there is any kind of trauma for the mother, if there is a physiological imbalance, if it is difficult for the breathing experience, if there is any problem with the flow of nutrients to the body, if the mother is under even occasional acute emotional stress, then you will make an attempt to pull back away from the body, in an attempt to rediscover the realm of Spirit. When you do this, the body of the fetus goes numb, that is, *life force* is withdrawn from it. And as it grows, the nervous system adapts to the level of *life force* that is flowing through it, and that is what comes from you and not from another. So that anytime during this period of nine months, you are in a particular universe, you're having physical experience, not unlike one who is sixty years old in the physical dimension. You are experiencing the sensory realm of third-dimensionality. And you are already being deeply influenced by psychic patterns not your own.

Therefore, the journey of awakening requires, from the moment of birth on, the development of certain motor skills, certain verbal skills, certain social skills, so that hopefully, if you're very lucky, by the time you're about twenty or twenty-one years of age, you're ready to start finding out who *you* are. It is very, very rare for an individual, especially in your cultural time frame, to emerge at the age of ten or twelve or fourteen or seventeen with a deep sense of themselves *apart from* the parents, the family or the culture. You *think* you are yourself, but you are really a *bundle of reactivity* seeking to find approval, seeking to find safety, survival, friendship—*in the world*. That is, you are already caught up in the perception that what you experience is coming *to* you from the *outside*, and that you must, therefore, seek to adapt yourself to it. *You are not yet alive.*

If you are very, very fortunate, during the time frame of the twenties, you merely experience greater degrees of freedom, greater degrees of making your own decisions and experiencing the outcomes. This can be a very turbulent time. Still, you will *believe* that you know yourself, and yet you have not even begun to know yourself. And again, this is for the majority.

As you go into your thirties, there is an opportunity now. Spirit begins to speak to you. Situations begin to emerge that require of you deeper understanding. If you're very, very fortunate, you will have begun to realize the great influence that the parents have had. Usually, this is a state of rebellion. Internally, you will begin to individuate more clearly. The *spiritual search* often begins in the thirties in earnest. You may have been aware of that earlier in the twenties. Again, this is not a hard and fast rule, but generally, by the thirties, it is time to *truly, truly* begin to answer the yearning of the soul.

Now, if the egoic consciousness has been fundamentally successful, that is, you've found a way to create your survival, you've developed what are called the personalities that allow you to interact with the insanity of the third-dimensional human realm, if you've had no major calamities or traumas, if you've had no major failures, you might continue into your forties with the smugness of thinking that you've got it all together. If you have found ways to avoid the fundamental gnawing question:

> *What is my purpose? Why have I really come to this planet? I am more than just this. I am Pure Soul. I am Pure Spirit. I know there's more to it than this . . .*

If you've been able to successfully keep yourself distracted, that question may not yet have fully arisen.

The egoic consciousness is merely that part of the body-mind that is responsible for keeping you physically alive. It is fueled by the desire for survival, the desire for safety. It wishes to create a certain set of order around you, because through order it can anticipate what will be required to keep the physiological organism functioning.

Now, what occurs is that somewhere along the line, usually very, very early in life, you begin to identify with the egoic mind and include your psychic state, your mental perceptions. The *ideas* you begin to learn about the world begin to be enfolded in the physiological individual, which is really the home of the ego. *The body is the home of the ego*, the body-mind, including the brain structure and the higher dimensions of functionality of the body, which is all the brain is, just a higher level of organizational principles and characteristics—to do what? To help the body function.

So a further step of forgetting who you are occurs when you begin to sense yourself as *identified with* the particular perceptions, the particular belief structures, that are floating around in the higher mind of the body, itself. You have forgotten the soul. You have forgotten Spirit. You've become identified as an American, as an Afro-American, as a Caucasian, as a boy, as a girl, as a fan of some sports team, as a lover of ice cream. You begin to take on and create what are called *principles*, never realizing that the principles often are merely the *product,* or the outcome, of your *social learning* from the time you were in the womb, and from the time that you were *conditioned* by the schooling of your culture.

Many of you have gone so far as to believe that you are an Alabaman, or a Washingtonian, or a Californian, because someone has told you that that's where you live. And though you've never found a boundary upon the face of the Earth that says,

Here is California and here is Nevada,

you have found a sign that someone has created and you have read it, and believed it, and have created an *identification* with one small aspect of life. Many of you are only now emerging to sense yourself as a *global citizen,* something that transcends being an American or a Canadian or a South African or a Russian.

So you begin to sense, by what we're sharing, this process whereby you keep making yourself smaller and smaller and smaller and smaller, taking on psychic patterns from the parents, from the peers, from the society around you. The spiritual path begins when, for some reason, something begins to whisper to you,

> *This is not who you are. This is not why you've come.*
> *You've come to heal your sense of separation from*
> *God. You've come to realize the Truth.*

Egoic consciousness, then, begins with the *shock* at
the moment of conception that brings your attention
to be completely fixated on, and as, the physiological
form beginning to emerge from a certain web of
relationship. This begins to *color* your vision, *color* your
understanding. It gives you your unique individuality
in the world. As you grow, as you emerge, as you move
through certain experiences, you become *colored*
by what you've had to do to survive. You become
colored by the psychic imprints of those around you.
You think you're thinking your own thoughts, when
what is often the case is that you're merely parroting
all that has come into your computer bank, into the
brain and into the body.

Now, it is quite true that this all began because there
was a *resonance* between the web of relationships of
the parents, and of the society, and where your own
unique quality of consciousness was, prior to birth. In
this sense, karma can be said to exist. Karma simply
means *action, the effect of,* so that when you drop a
pebble in the pond, you create a certain ripple. As
long as you continue that ripple, by dropping the
same pebble in the pond, you get the same results.
And part of those results is the need to be identified
with only this vibrational field of energy called
physicality.

Until you decide to *change the momentum* of the

ripples you are creating in the depth of the mind, you cannot begin to *ascend* from the third dimension. The desire to do so is always within you. That is, it may be dormant, but the desire to know God must *necessarily* be within each soul, since God is your Reality. You have fallen asleep, and at some point, there comes the urge to awaken. When it comes, it is *unmistakable*. The fireworks may not occur, but a *shift happens* within your beingness and you *know* that you can never return to the way it was. You can never again *pretend* that life is only what you see through the senses.

Now, the soul begins to speak. The connection that was once lost begins to be reestablished. It was never really lost, it was just forgotten, it was suppressed. It became the background instead of the foreground. It begins to whisper in the depth of your being. It comes to you in the form of your dreams. You begin to notice books that you never noticed before. You might wander into your New Age section of the bookstore, not even understanding what compelled you to do so. And there, you pick up a copy of *The Jeshua Letters*, or *A Course in Miracles*, or some other such book, that begins to trigger within you a *thirst* and a *longing*. A friend suddenly invites you to come to some funny workshop, the kind you've never been to before. And yet, when you go, something triggers you, something touches you. Something begins to awaken. You may not notice it, but it actually triggers a physiological state within the body, within what is called the *chakra system*. The *heart* begins to stir in its slumber. And the mind *thirsts* for *knowledge*, a knowledge unlike any that it has gathered in its identification with egoic consciousness.

The longing to awaken has come. And from this moment, though you don't understand it, you begin to attract, slowly at first, perhaps stumbling a bit now and then, exactly those situations that will keep prodding you to look deeper. A meditation teacher comes. A prayer group comes that you feel called to join. You begin the process of your study. And a new question is emerging.

No longer,

> *How can I survive?*

No longer,

> *How can I make money? How can I do all these things?*

A new question comes:

> *Who am I?*

There may be many forms to it, but the question remains one:

> *Who am I? What am I? From where have I come?*
> *What is life . .*
> *God? What is God? How can there be anything at all?*

These questions begin to stir in the mind. Often they first make their appearance in some form around the age of ten to twelve, as you enter into a stage of life that is your first taste of *individuation*. That is, you begin to sense that you are—just like when the child was born, it began to sense that it was *other than* the mother's body—at around the age of ten to twelve you begin to sense that you are *other than* the mother/father, that there's something that wants to think for itself and be for itself. Often those questions will begin to come, that's the first stirring. *Usually*, those questions are not attended to. There's much too much else to do. You still need to learn to think. You still need to learn to drive a car. You still need to learn to balance a checkbook.

Later, those questions occur again, generally in the early to mid-twenties. But again, the momentum is to become established as a physiological being, and so the questions are suppressed. Into the thirties, and most definitely by the forties, those questions begin to press up upon the consciousness. You know how to make money. You know how to balance a checkbook. You've done these things in the world. You've had sex, you've baked cakes, hmm? You've thrown birthday parties. You've gotten drunk. You've done it all, hmm? But something else is gnawing—something else is gnawing.

This is also a point of great challenge:

> *What will I be committed unto—Love or fear? Will fear run me? Will the very principles that I've identified myself with, and have utilized to ensure my survival, my ordering of life—will these things become more important than realizing the Self?*

Hmm? Awakening the Christ within. For you see, awakening requires a *dismantling* of the structures of consciousness by which you've been ordering your perceptions of the third dimension. Ultimately, to truly awaken completely requires the dismantling of very subtle, deeply embedded patterns of perception that were already making up the soul *prior to* your incarnation in this life. The slate must be wiped clean so that all that remains is the Reality of Spirit, with no filament or trace of egoic consciousness left. That is not an easy thing to do, yet it requires no effort, save the effort to Love. Love is the great healer. Love—that which erases the imprints in the depth of the soul.

The patterns that you brought forth with you as a soul are like a magnet, that is, they attract energy states in the physical dimension experience that are resonant with those patterns. Often, when you say you "fall in love," it's just that you've come into contact with another field of energy that happens to fit, hand-in-glove, with the very patterns of consciousness that you carry in the depth of your being. Old memories of other incarnations are triggered when you visit a certain physical location. And the emotion feels so good and warm in the heart,

> *Surely this is where I must live on this planet. This is with whom I must spend my life.*

Hmm? And yet, all of it is emerging as the result of your *karma,* that is, the *patterns* and the *effects* that have come from those patterns.

Awakening does require *vigilance.* Awakening requires that rather than merely going with the reactions of the third-dimensional being, you begin to *question,* you begin to *observe,* you begin to *feel,* you begin to *think* more deeply. You begin to engage yourself in some form of spiritual practice. And whether it be meditation or prayer – or what have you—all of these things are modalities which *interrupt* the *momentum* of the soul, which is normally caught up with its third-dimensional experience. You interrupt the pattern of being caught up in the world long enough to sit quietly for half an hour, or to chant, or to walk—you do *something* in a different way. You're beginning to *turn the momentum of the mind back upon itself*. You're beginning to become *self-observant* rather than *world observant*.

Now, for all of you that would like to quicken and hasten that process, the answer is very simple: *spend more time becoming self-observant*; less time being concerned with what's going on in the world; and *no* time blaming the world for your state of being—not parents, not society, not God—but *owning*. And here is an important word that we will share with you. You've heard it many times before, but when you truly reach a point of assuming one hundred percent—all—*responsibility* for what you think, what you feel, what you see, what you experience, this creates a *quantum leap* in the other direction, toward self-observation, toward the freedom that you are seeking, toward the healing of the soul, toward the realization of your purpose, toward freedom, toward awakening. Without it, the spiritual journey never quite gets off the ground—you could say almost literally! You never quite ascend, and indeed you cannot ascend, without the *assumption of complete responsibility*. You must extricate yourself from the psychic enmeshment with other webs of relationship in the sense that you've come to perceive that *they* are *causing* your decisions. In other words, *you must assume power.*

You are well aware of those in your third-dimensional reality who assume power. You sometimes love them or loathe them, but they are powerful. Can you assume the same power in your own life? Can you come to look at your beloved, if you're in relationship, and say:

> *You know something, this being is not causing how I feel. This being can never fulfill me. This being has nothing that I can extricate from them in order to fill up my sense of lack. I am alone in my journey to God, for I abide alone in God. That is, I'm an individuated spark of divinity. It's within me. The Kingdom of Heaven is within me. What I am seeking is within me. What fulfills me must come forth from within.*

This is why once I said,

> *If you do not bring forth what is within you, what is within you will destroy you. If you bring forth what is within you, what is within you will save you.*

If you do not bring forth what is within you—and what is within you is Love, is Christ—you will feel burdened and unfulfilled. And usually, most human beings go through their entire life with a sense of unfulfillment, lamenting what the world has done *to them*, lamenting the decisions and choices they've made in the past. They become burdened by what is on the outside, along with what is in the past. And eventually the body dies, the spirit withers on the vine. And at death, another quantum leap occurs that is *shocking* as they discover themselves to be popped back into another vibrational state that often triggers great fear.

Very few beings upon your human plane have entered death *consciously*. It is indeed time, even for those of you that listen to this tape, to simply make a decision:

> *I will enter into the transition, called death, with deliberate consciousness. I will make sure, by beginning now, that I carry no resentment, that I have forgiven everyone of everything. And as the body does enter that state, I will release the world and require nothing of it. I will not long to run off in freedom, but I will experience death consciously. I'll notice the subtle energy changes as I flip from this dimension into another at the speed of Light.*

Beloved friends, come to understand, at this stage of our journey together, the *true immensity* of *who you are* and *what you are*. That you are not so much dealing with "things" in the world as *patterns of energy* that reflect in some way what is already occurring in *your* consciousness. If you're experiencing things in the third-dimensional plane, it can mean only that *you* have chosen to vibrate at a certain frequency—or otherwise, you couldn't have the experience. You couldn't have the experience of running into a wall with your body unless you were vibrating at the same rate as the wall.

Is it possible to change the vibrational frequency of the physical body? Listen very carefully. I'm going to say something rather unique. I'm going to say, no. It is only possible to change the vibrational frequency of your *consciousness, out of which* the body has emerged.

This requires a *turning about in the seat of the soul*, a changing of the momentum of consciousness—not outward, but *inward*. Not as an *escape* from the world—it isn't something you have to do all day, everyday. But you spend time in prayer and meditation. You spend time in forgiveness. You spend time breathing and relaxing. You begin to allow changes to occur in the choices you are making, so they come more into alignment with your growing understanding of yourself as a creator, as a soul. You begin to change your environment. You paint the color of the walls of your bedroom a different color, that which brings a sense of pleasantness to you. You change your physical environment completely by moving into a different apartment. Many of you know perfectly well that often it means the changing of relationships. And initially, this does make sense.

But there is a *point* in which you realize that you could keep changing relationships *ad nauseum* and never get anywhere—that now it's time to *settle down*, be with the one you're with—or the ones you're with—and yet utilize your time with them to discover what *patterns* have been running you. *Self-awareness* . . . turning the momentum of the mind back toward the Self

> *Why do I think what I think? Why did I see what I saw? Why did I react the way that I reacted?*

Eventually, the soul that is *truly committed* to awakening

does not flee uncomfortable situations until it believes it has fully extracted all the wisdom that it can. There is a way of knowing when that occurs, and we'll get to that at a later time. In short, when there is just a quiet sense of peace, and you can look upon the players in the experiences you've just had with perfect equanimity and see them as perfectly innocent, and you detect that there is nothing in the body that is not at peace—the heart is not racing, the shoulders are not tight—you truly understand that you are not in fear, then it is time to move on. If there is *reactivity* in the mind because of anything that emerges in your relationship with your brothers or sisters, rest assured, the lesson is not complete. If your "principles" have been "violated," rest assured, there is much to be learned.

Remember always, that all events are *neutral.* And in a large measure, the process of awakening is a process whereby you *dissolve the value* you have placed upon certain ideas and perceptions of what life is and what life is for. Yes, there are times you will be troubled, as you come to realize that what you *thought* the world was for, and everything you've been putting your energy into, means *nothing.* Often, this precipitates a period of what has been called by certain mystics the *Dark Night of the Soul.* It's really not the Dark Night of the Soul. It's the *Dark Night of the Ego,* and the *Healing of the Soul.*

The Way of Transformation requires *utmost personal responsibility, utmost personal dedication.* No one can do it for you. And the patterns you feel weighed down by, the fears that are yet within the mind, will remain with you for all of eternity—until you decide to *heal* them. From that desire you will attract the situations, the teachers, the books, the experiences that provide for you the opportunity to do so. There is an acceleration of the healing process *only when* you *completely release* any valuation on victimhood—that is, the belief that,

> *Somehow, in some way, someone or something has done something to me.*

Now, that's a simple thought to hear, and one can nod their head. It is another thing to look *honestly* upon your reactions in life to make sure that you are not, at any time, perceiving yourself as a victim. The practice of extending Love can often teach you that this is so. When you take a situation that pushes your buttons, and you decide to not flee, but stay, this teaches you the Truth of your Reality.

This is why the practice of forgiveness is so *extraordinarily valuable.* In fact, you could say that, ultimately, the practice of forgiveness is the whole of spirituality, since forgiveness means to let the world off the hook, to step out of any sense of victim consciousness, and then even beyond that, to *forgive one's self* for the perceptions made in error—perceptions of one's brothers and sisters, of the world, and of God. Ultimately, forgiveness is forgiveness of one's self for ever allowing delusion to settle into one's own mind, whereby one perceived one's self as separate from God, separate from brothers and sisters, capable of being victimized. Forgiveness, when completed, *is* the establishment of Love.

Beloved friends, look well, then, to see,

> *Where am I perceiving myself as a victim of the world I see? Am I feeling constrained in my relationship? Do I resent my spouse?*

The spouse is not holding you where you are. And that one does not have the power to take from you your ability to look with Love upon her or him.

Is it your job you hate? No one forces you to drive your car upon the freeway to arrive at your place of employment—no one.

> *Oh, but I must survive!*

Then you have made yourself a victim of the perception of the need to survive. Any one of you at any time is perfectly free to drop the valuation you have placed upon the world.

I was once criticized for dropping the valuation that my particular society had sought to implant within me, the valuation that said that a son should follow in the footsteps of the father, that if the father is a carpenter, then you've got to take over the family business. I said,

> *I must be about my Father's business.*

And I spoke, of course, of my Heavenly Father. I had to know the Truth of who I was, and my purpose was to awaken Christ. I broke the mores, the rules, of the family structure within that community, within that time frame. Like many of you, I was a bit of a rebel. And where other children were conforming to the pressures of society, I went off to study with the rabbis and teachers, to sit in the desert at night, often not to return. Even at the age of twelve I separated myself from my parents at the time of a great festival, and went to hang out in my Father's house and talk with the spiritual leaders.

Are *you* willing to break with the conventions of the world in which you live? This can be as simple as, instead of gathering with friends to watch movies on Saturday night, you say,

> *No, I'm going to go into my closet and light a candle and pray . . . for six hours.*

And when they look at you with their eyebrows raised, you simply smile.

In what ways are you conforming to the views others hold of you and *their* need to have you be a certain way? Do you show up at the aunt's birthday party just because the family says you always should, yet in your *heart* you have no desire to? The willingness to trust and follow your heart, not the reactive ego that is often interpreted to be the heart, but the heart that longs to know God—this is a telltale sign of whether or not one is achieving maturity. Beloved friends, look well, in this *Way of Transformation*, for you *must discover* any corner of the mind that is yet holding out the view that life is something which happens *to* you, and that there is something you are helpless to change. The position of being a victim is a position of loss of power. And Christ is not about loss of power. Ultimately, it is not so much about going anywhere, as much as it is about abiding within, realizing that this world is unreal, this world is harmless. And in any situation, it is *you* with all power under Heaven and Earth to teach only Love.

But that requires, you see, that you let the world off the hook, that no one and nothing is any longer responsible for your joy, your happiness and your peace. For you have established your unity with Spirit, with God. You've realized the Self, and you look out with equanimity upon a neutral world. And as this physical universe fades from view for the final time, within you will be no compulsion to avoid it, or to enter it, for you will be free—free even as you walk this Earth. The body moves, the soul does not. The mind thinks, but the *depth* of the mind is as still as the ocean. You live, yet not you, for Christ dwells in you. And wherever you go, the presence of peace enters the room before you. You are awake, you are free—all because once you made a decision to give up victimhood, and to assume responsibility for learning how, in all situations, to be only the presence of Love.

So, again you can see that we've made a bit of a continuation. And we will continue to continue until what has occurred within your consciousness is that you have begun to remember the journey that you have taken.

Turn back, then, toward your creations. If there is anything uncomfortable about your past, *turn back to it, examine it, feel it,* look at all the patterns that made it come up. Look at the choices you've made that, perhaps now, you are embarrassed about. But look not upon them with judgment. Look with curiosity.

Learn to look with wonder and the innocence of a child:

> *Well, that was an interesting decision I made, when I was twelve, to steal my neighbor's bicycle. I remember how I ended up in juvenile hall. Hmm . . . what was going on just before I made that decision? What pattern was running me? Oh, my goodness! I was looking to get attention from my Dad. Wow! So the need for approval was running me. How fascinating! How is that pattern running me now? Is there any trace of it left—still needing approval of another?*

I say this unto you: Every moment of experience you've ever had is *available* for you, right down to the moment of conception, right down to the quantum leap that you took from a certain vibrational frequency into this physical domain. *Self-awareness is everything*, for it is the Self with a capital S that you most long to realize.

Beloved friends, we love you, but we *cannot* make your journey for you. We can only walk with you on the way that you choose. You can utilize your relationship with me and with Shanti Christo to fully awaken. Or, you can come close, and then decide it's uncomfortable, and run away again. You will only run to another structure or form of energy, a web of relationships, that forces you to stay with what is uncomfortable in order to learn, in order to grow, in order to heal, *in order to Love*—not as a cursory,

> *Oh well, yes, I love you.*

No—but something done *whole-bodily* in which

there is no longer any reactivity filtering through the nervous system of the body-brain. For the ultimate state of consciousness is not an aversion of this world, but the *embracing* of this world. There is no greater sense of freedom than to be able to abide where you are as one who is free.

Be you, therefore, at peace this day, beloved friends.

Be you, therefore, at peace always.

Amen.

Lesson Six

Now, we begin.

And once again, greetings unto you, beloved and holy friends. Once again, we come forth to abide with you from that place which has never truly been left. Once again, we come forth to abide with you, not as those that are apart from you, but as those who love you, as those who walk with you on the way that you have chosen; as those who have sent forth the call to awaken, to heal, to arise, to welcome Love into every dark corner where once the ego had sought authority.

We come forth because we love you, and we come forth because we are Love. And above all, remember always, we come forth because Love is eternally attracted to its own. And we are attracted unto you because you are that Love, sent forth as a ray of Light from the Holy Mind of God, not to suffer the world, not to become identified with illusion, but to transform each illusion, through the constant practice of your remembering:

> *I and my Father are One. Only Love is real, and Love, alone, heals. And my commitment is to the Reality of Love. And therefore, Father, bring each moment to me that I might learn, anew, to Love, and allow that Love to transform a temporary illusion into that which extends the good, the holy, and the beautiful.*

Herein lies your purpose. Herein lies your function, and *herein*—and only here—is Life.

Therefore, indeed, it is with great joy that we come forth to abide with you who are sent forth from the Holy Mind of God, even as we are! For we are joined eternally. And separation *cannot* exist. That Love, then, which has given birth to all things is within you now. All universes arise within you. All of Creation waits on your welcome.

And herein lies the continuation of the theme which we have begun to speak with you about. *All* of Creation waits on *your* welcome. And Creation does not wait to swallow you. Creation does not wait to prove to you that you live in an unloving universe. Creation does not wait for you to be as a brick wall upon which you may hit the head. Creation does not wait upon you to scuttle your dreams and your plans. Creation is innocent. Creation—and listen very carefully—is utterly powerless. It *becomes* powerful according to that which *you* give unto it—the value, the meaning, the purpose, and the function. These things come not from Creation, Itself, but rather, they are extended to It, they flow to It, they penetrate Creation through the minds (which share one Mind) of each and every one of you.

This is why it is absolutely *impossible* to look upon anything which is outside of yourself. And the great glory of the time given unto you, the time you experience as a body-mind upon an apparent planet, upon an apparent physical universe—the great glory and gift of time is that you remain infinitely free to decide how *you* will choose to perceive Creation, and therefore imbue It with the power that either reflects illusion and the creations of fear, or extends the *good*, the *holy*, and the *beautiful*.

Each time you think a loving thought, you have literally blessed all infinite realms of Creation. Each time you have become unwittingly identified with a fearful thought, you have separated yourself from the Perfect Love of God, and you have denied yourself your function. And here we're using the term 'separation' slightly differently, in that it creates the illusion within your mind that there is something you *must* separate from in order to find your safety, your invulnerability.

The function of the Holy Child of God remains eternally one: to bless Creation and, thereby, restore It to the perfect reflection of God's presence. And God is but Love. Love, then, embraces all things, trusts all things. Love—*Love*—is the nature of your being. And when you finally choose to awaken wholly, by welcoming Love back into your mind, and by becoming committed to resting *only* in loving thoughts, you will discover that illusions are just that—they contain no existence. And you have been resting in the Holy Mind of God, eternally.

Creation, then, waits on your welcome. Creation *waits* for *you* to embrace it. Creation *waits* upon *you*, the holy, anointed Child of God, sent as that one who is the savior of all things. You are, then, the messiah. You are, then, Christ Incarnate . . . to the degree that you become crazy enough in the eyes of your world to simply assume the Truth and become wholly committed to listening to no other voice. For there is given unto you one Teacher, even that that I have called the Comforter, the Holy Spirit, the Voice for God, placed within your mind, in the very moment you first dared to dream the thought of separation, of guilt. And *guilt is the mother of fear.*

Beloved friends, take a moment and just for the fun of it, practice making a simple decision. This takes no effort since you do it all the time, anyway. You're already a master of this. In this simple decision, observe the place you are *now.* If you are alone, or seem to be alone through the physical eyes, look at the so-called objects around you. Feel the temperature of the air. Hear the sounds that come in through the ears. If you are with others, include your brothers and sisters in your observation. Decide to look upon all these things with perfect innocence. And say within the mind—which is to use the power of the mind to literally create perception—simply say, as you look at each object or person,

> *I do not know what this is for. I do not know what my brother or sister needs.*

And realize that it is not necessary to know, to interpret, to analyze. Your function is to bless Creation with the Reality of the Love of Christ. And yet, that blessing will hold no power until you return to the beginning. And the beginning is just that state of unknowing, of *not* knowing, of realizing your *complete ignorance.* For Christ does not store perceptions and knowledge. Christ, eternally in love with all that God is, merely *opens, receives,* and *gives,* knowing that that which is given comes not of him or herself, but rather *through* him or herself, from Infinite Mystery that I have called Abba, or Father.

When you decide to fully accept the one purpose given to you in reality, there will be nothing that will block your way. Every step you take will, literally, take you through obstacles that dissolve as you approach them. For because you abide in the Mind of God, *you know no limitation.* And the realm of what appears to be illusion, of solid matter, of people with different opinions, holds no power to prevent you from bringing forth the blessing that heals all illusion.

Creation, then, waits on your welcome. And that, then, requires that you choose to look upon all things in the world (and in a moment we're going to talk a little bit more about what the world really is), you choose to look upon all things of the world and forgive it. And why? Because until forgiveness is genuine, embracing is not possible. The attempt to embrace Creation, while judgment is still held in the mind, merely brings what you would call in your world, a great frustration. It is like reaching for the carrot at the end of the stick and never being able to reach it. And that is why we have spoken so much about the importance of forgiveness. It dissolves the barrier of fear between you and what you have come to perceive as other than, or outside, yourself. Forgiveness is the *bridge* that brings Creation to you, and you to It. And when you have joined with It through forgiveness, now the embrace is easy, for that Creation rests in the palm of your hand.

Creation waits upon *you* because *It* is powerless. Being the extension or the reflection of thought, you are the literal creator of the world. That world exists nowhere, save within your own mind. Therefore, what world must you embrace? Must you travel to some ancient monastery fifty thousand miles around the planet somewhere, two or three times, in order to find the Creation that waits on your welcome? No. Must you go anywhere to discover the ability to bless and heal Creation? No. The world which waits on your welcome is, quite literally, *the thoughts and perceptions which you discover streaming through the field of your unique awareness*, and that is all.

Beloved friends, there *is* nothing outside of you. And if you would know your Father's Will for you, merely look upon what is arising within your own mind as a perception, and ask only this:

> *Am I willing* now *to use time constructively to embrace this creation passing through the field of my awareness, and bless it with the perfect Love of Christ?*

To first embrace it through forgiveness, which returns it to its neutrality and powerlessness, and *then*, through that embrace, to bless it, and thereby dissolve the illusory power that it seemed to hold.

As you choose to truly practice being the presence of Christ, as you cultivate the practice of blessing the world, you will discover a very interesting thing. You would swear that many of the thoughts, or what seem to be experiences, or emotions, that are passing through your screen of awareness, don't seem to have any causal link to anything you've experienced in your current life time. And for those of you that have done the inner work necessary to create a transparency of the barrier between lifetimes, you won't even find, necessarily, a causal link between the world, the creation that is passing through the field of your awareness, and anything you have *ever* experienced as a unique ray of Light.

And why is this important? Simply because the human mind tends to take the whole process of awakening far too *personally*. In Reality, there is nothing that is personal. There is only Christ, as God's true and only Creation, and the field of illusion that has been birthed through the freedom of that Mind when once it thought,

I wonder if I can create something unlike God?

Those are the only two options—Love or fear, Reality or illusion.

Therefore, all that you see that is unlike Love is merely a passing phenomenon, arising within the Holy Mind of Christ as a temporary attempt to do something different than what Christ is created for. Therefore, when anything arises within the mind, it is truly not necessary to analyze it. Certainly, don't argue for it. But rather, come back to the point of *ignorance* . . .

I do not know what this thought, or this image, or this emotion, or this memory—whatever it is—is for. But I do know one thing: I have made a commitment to reawaken as Christ. And therefore, I will use this one moment, this one thought, *this one passing phenomenon, to practice what I was created for—to bless creation, and thereby transform it into that which extends* the good, *the* holy, *and the* beautiful . . . *infinitely, eternally, with joy, with innocence, with graciousness, with peace.*

. . . with *marvel* at the Great Mystery that Love Is, that your Father Is!

As you come to truly understand how simple your task is, your burden will become lighter, for you will discover that you cannot help but be in the right place at the right time. And those committed to awakening to God recognize the great gift of each moment:

> Here *is my Father's Will, right before me.* This *is the moment that is* crying *for Love.*

And this is the moment that will be repeated *ad nauseum* until *somebody* decides to bless it. It might as well be you!

Creation, then, waits upon your welcome by merely holding the thought:

> *Okay, it's all arising within me anyway. I've tried in a million ways to avoid it and get away from it, and yet it seems to follow me wherever I go. I might as well sit down on the park bench, have a nice cold glass of water, listen to the birds sing, and simply bless Creation.*

Now, many of you are not yet to the point of truly transcending, or creating the transparency of, what you have identified as your "personal stuff," that which makes up the "I" within the phenomenal world. That's okay. As you simply practice blessing the world as it arises in your awareness, that very sense of I becomes increasingly transparent until it simply dissolves away in Light, as though it had never been. In the meantime, come back to what we shared earlier. Time is given to you that you might use it constructively. Therefore, do not seek to trample what you call the ego, or the sense of a personal self. It's simply there. *It is* what is arising. Are you willing to bless it?

As you then, as a soul, already dreaming the dream of separation, begin to create the phenomena of what you perceive to be separate lifetimes, falling into the condensation or density of physicality, we have shared with you that patterns begin to settle into the nervous system of the body and the mind. Belief systems not yours, but rather coming from the field of the parents and of the culture and the time frame into which you have incarnated, literally imprint themselves in the mind, and in the literal nervous system of the body. These are what you might call *cellular imprints.* Your creation waits on your welcome. Therefore, can you turn back to the body-mind? Can you turn back to your very memories that seem to be associated with an individual self, with a personal history, and rather than trying to pretend that that's not there, simply recognize if that is how you are perceiving yourself, *bring Love to that?* Stop trying to shake the ego off as though you could shake your hand off of your arm!

Those that choose to turn back and look upon their experience within the singular field of one body-mind arising, from the moment of conception as you know it, unto the present of where you find yourself, at whatever age, are already engaged in the highest work of Christ. For they are choosing to turn back and embrace Creation by looking upon ancient memories, and no longer fearing them, but allowing them to be brought into the awareness, by whatever means, so that that memory can be blessed, transformed, healed, released.

Beloved friends, fear of turning about, if you would perceive it—looking backwards into time, into your seemingly personal experience—can seem horrifying. And yet I say unto you, the sense of horror that many of you feel is not linked to the memories themselves. It is *only* linked to what you have decided to *believe* about the memory, and nothing else. Begin, then, by *forgiving yourself your past*. Look upon the objects, just as we did with the initial meditation or exercise. Look upon the objects that are the memories of your past and say within the mind:

> *I forgive you. You are perfectly neutral. And I choose now to remember you, to re-member, to embrace again, that I might bless you.*

And with that blessing release the terror, the hurt, the judgment, the fear, the incredible dramas you seem to have dreamt. And by releasing that burden of illusion, that memory becomes as a crystal, as a gem given unto you as part of an infinite journey that seems to be yours, but truly belongs to everyone . . . transformed and purified because *you brought Christ to illusion* in order that Creation might be transformed.

I want to, then, offer unto you—those that would be willing to do this—a simple exercise. It will take you thirty days, if you apply yourself daily. This need not take more than perhaps ten or fifteen minutes. Merely come to your chair, your place of devotion, your place of meditation or prayer, and begin with the exercise of abiding as Christ for five minutes. When that is completed, then simply continue by recognizing that you do not know what a single thing is or what it's for, that you do not know what a single brother or sister, now in your life or who has crossed your path, has ever truly needed. Admit your ignorance. And then simply and deliberately say within the mind,

> *I choose to forgive the creation which will now be brought into my awareness. Holy Spirit, what is in need of my blessing?*

And as you sit observing what comes into the *field of the mind*, the *field of awareness*, it may in fact be a sudden tightness in a muscle. Do not overlook it, for even that is arising within the field of mind. Be with whatever that creation seems to be—a picture, a memory, a feeling, a thought, a sensation in the body. Be with it. Single it out and stay with it. Look upon it and, once again, practice forgiveness in this simple way:

> *Object of creation, I forgive you the judgment I have placed upon you. And thereby it is released. Now do I embrace you.*

And literally feel yourself, if those that wish to visualize might see themselves as taking a hand, and wrapping it around that thought, that object, that memory, that sensation in the muscle—lovingly, gently, as though you were holding the most delicate of flowers, the most beautiful flower ever created, a gift directly from God. Look upon that object and simply say:

> *I am Christ, and in this moment I use time to its greatest glory. Beloved object, I bless you. I embrace you. I heal you.*

Then, if it is a picture in the mind, a thought, simply allow it to be dissolved. And notice that as that image dissolves, you will detect that there is a *field of spacious peace* that you may not have noticed was there. The object of creation has simply become *transparent* to the Reality of who you truly are, for peace *is* the nature of Christ.

Do this as long as it is comfortable and the mind does not seem to waver or get too rattled. If it seems to become uncomfortable, simply notice that discomfort, acknowledge and thank yourself for your little willingness to heal Creation. Let the exercise go, and be about your day. Come back to this exercise as often as you wish, but at least once a day for each of the next thirty days.

Many of you will begin to see a certain pattern emerging. That is, many of the objects that come for healing may seem to be almost chronologically linked to your experience in this life. Others of you may notice that you are tapping into a multitude of other lifetimes. And some of you will experience and realize that over this thirty days, nothing seemed to show up with which you could link a personal causation, but rather, it seems to be presented to you by something else, and it is coming from some unknown dimension of the universe.

Never judge what you see, what you feel, or the thought that arises. There are many dimensions of Creation, many forms of life, many ways in which experience is created. Do not judge what you see, what you think, what you feel. But hold it as an object that has been brought to you by the Holy Spirit who is asking you, as Christ, to bring the healing of blessing to it.

Many of you will have very profound insights and realizations over the next thirty days. Some of you will have memories come that you had never been able to access before. And why? Simply because there has been a barrier of fear, that's all. Fear is what creates and sustains the illusion of separation, so that when anyone says,

Gee, I can't remember back past the age of five,

that is utter nonsense. Every event you have ever known is present for you now, in its fullness. You've merely used selectivity, as a result of judgment and fear, to press down into your mind certain events.

As you approach it in the way that we have offered to you, you will discover that the fear of Creation seems to become more and more absent. Therefore, the barrier between yourself and Creation becomes more *transparent*. Some of you will even have very clear experiences of transcending all sense of personal consciousness and suddenly realizing that the vastness of your being is greater than your entire cosmos.

Some of you will experience improved relationships with a coworker, with an old friend, a sudden phone call or a letter from someone you haven't been in touch with—why? Because somewhere in the process, something bubbled up and was given to you for healing that literally sent the message to that one that you are with them, and that *they* can heal and release their own patterns. Remember that all minds are joined, so that as you are engaged in healing, you are providing a spark of Light that holds the potential to uplift *every mind* in your dimension, and in all dimensions.

We abide in a dimension of consciousness in which there are no barriers. Everything is perfectly transparent. We are very aware then, simply by selecting to turn our attention to whomever we wish, exactly what you are currently involved in healing. And rest assured, each time you choose a loving thought, each time you choose to join with us to be the Arisen Christ, *you* spark joy within *us*. For we are embracing with you, in delight, your choice for healing.

Separation cannot exist. Your healing brings *us* joy. So now the 'cat' must come out of the bag. We truly come to you and help you heal for very selfish reasons. We know that as you heal, *our* joy is uplifted and extended. And we know that as you heal, you come closer and closer and closer to remembering that you are all that we are—already. While we play in a dimension that seems to not include physicality, and you seem to play in a dimension that does include physicality, as you become transparent to Creation, the sense of separation dissolves, and more and more and more and more we *dance together* in the eternal joy of the Atonement, bringing Creation back to the Love of God, thereby transforming it, thereby illuminating it, thereby creating within Creation, Itself, the means by which the *good*, the *holy* and the *beautiful* is extended forever!

Suffering need not be. The suffering with which you may yet be identified—*this need not be.* It is only by *choice* that suffering is held in the mind. And it is only by *choice* that it can be healed and released.

Beloved friends—friends *indeed*, for we take with great sincerity the use of that word—we are, indeed, with you always. Please notice, then, that in this hour we have chosen to transmit the thought "we," rather than "I." For although the one that you have identified as Jeshua is very much part of this communion, this process of communication, please understand that no one heals alone. The extension of the good, the holy, and the beautiful is never done alone. *Creation is a collaboration.* And this is why *relationship* is the means of your salvation. *All healing involves the whole of Creation.*

We come to you because we love you. You may wish to look upon us and use the term *lineage*, if you wish. For within the resonances of beings within the dramas of creation, and within the dreams of separation, and in the infinite number of worlds that have arisen and continue to arise, a *resonance* has been created through an infinite number of souls that seem to be discrete and individual. And therefore, we are merely those who seem to have gone ahead of you a little bit in time, and seem to have awakened more thoroughly than you give yourself credit for in this moment. In Truth, the awakening has already occurred, it is already done. You are merely remembering the process of awakening.

We come, then, to you, as you would wish to perceive us. Some of you see us as far above you. Some see us as right next to you. Some believe you could never be equal to us—never so grand, never so great.

Some look at us and smile and say,

> *Would you move over and let me get on with this?*

All perception still falls within the realm of illusion.

Truth comes by *revelation*.

> *I and my Father are One!*

is only the utterance of inadequate words pointing to, or reflecting, a certain revelation of Truth.

We love you because you *are* who we are! And in the end, there is only Christ loving Christ back into wholeness—a wholeness that was never truly lost in the first place. And in that moment when Creation is returned, *you* have a good laugh:

> *I'll be darned! I never really went anywhere at all. And my brothers and sisters are with me here, and they are who I am.*

Remember, then, that each *loving* thought restores you to your rightful place. Every *fearful* thought merely delays the moment of your release and the restoration of your perfect peace. Remember that only Love can heal. No technique has ever brought healing, though it can provide a temporary field in which the mind can choose to love.

Remember how perfectly simple it is. It is not possible for you to be in the wrong place at the wrong time.

Imagine an employer who has decided to pay you one million of your golden coins per hour. And your only task is to place a flower where the employer wants it. And the way the employer works, because he likes to have fun, is to provide you an envelope, each day that you show up for work. And you open the envelope, and in it are a set of instructions:

> *Outside you will find a taxi cab. Take the taxi cab to the inner city, and there take up the job of the street sweeper. And on Tuesday morning, I'm going to send to you an eighty-four year old man who hates himself and feels himself to be useless. Give this man a beer, and sit down upon your curb and talk about how you used to hate yourself. It's okay if you never did, just do this for me. And as you talk, I will fill your mind with exactly the right words. And you will know just that time to turn and to look into that man's eyes and simply say, "Brother, you are loved." And healing will occur.*

Meanwhile, your coworker may just happen to get sent to a penthouse in what you call Paris, and there to eat the grandest of meals, there to be blessed with millions of golden coins surrounded by a harem of beautiful women or men, and the finest of wines. And yet it will all be a smoke screen so that when the room service person brings the next bottle of wine, I will whisper into their ear,

Bless that room service person.

Now, it looks, in the realm of form, as though there's a big difference between one blessed with infinite wealth hanging out in a penthouse in Paris, and one sitting on a lonely, cold curb in some deep, dark inner city, with an old man who hates himself. But I say unto you, *there is no difference.*

Now, there *is* no difference because Creation holds only *one* purpose, *one* goal, *one* value: *healing*—the healing that allows God's Holy Child, Christ, to arise from a useless dream and be restored to her rightful place at the right hand of God. That is not a spatial term. It simply means to think rightly, to be restored to sanity, so that Creation can flow forth ever more perfectly, ever more joyously, adding to the Kingdom by extending the increasingly *good*, the increasingly *holy*, the increasingly *beautiful*.

Never, then, judge yourself by comparison to another. Comparison and contrast is something that the egoic mind does, so that judgment can result—judgment of self, judgment of another—so that the dream of separation can continue. Since it is in the dream, it needs the dream to continue to maintain survival. Simply give it up. Each of you is as wealthy as the one next to you, for you *have* the Perfect Love of God. And you *are* as your Creator has created you to be: *unchanged, unchanging, and unchangeable, forever.* And no event has ever had an effect upon you. There is only Love, and You are That. Therefore, simply be who you are, and you *are* the Light that lights this world and restores it to the Loveliness of Heaven.

We would, then, begin to close this simple hour with this question for you to answer for yourself—not to discuss, not to analyze, not to ruminate over, but merely to sit in what appears to be your private realm and ponder, and to answer. For unless it is answered, there can be no movement. And *how* it is answered will determine your tomorrows. And you're going to have an infinite number of them, by the way.

The question is simply this: Do you recognize that you have already been every *where* and every *when* in the illusion of separation? Would you be willing, right now, in the quiet privacy of your own heart and mind, to use the Power of Awareness given unto you to *decide* to *be* Love?

Some of you will have just felt a feeling of fear come up. Some of you will feel a sudden thought rushing through your awareness,

Oh, this is a bunch of nonsense.

If you give the fear the power of reality, you will have effectively delayed the answering of the questions. If you listen to the thought that calls it "nonsense," you will have done the same thing. But the only thing you will have done is this, and please listen carefully: You will only have delayed a moment which will *not be forsaken.* You will have only delayed the inevitable, for your journey home has already long since begun.

And once *that* journey begins, rest assured, the end is certain. Push against it as you will, like a gnat shouting at the universe—

My *will be done, not God's!*

- and Love merely waits on your welcome.

Choose, then, beloved friends, to embrace the only answers those questions can have. For those answers are Truth, based on what is Real. And with your embracing of what is Real, the moment of your liberation is at hand. And Christ descends gently to begin to make Its home where once the illusion of a separate self once seemed to reign.

The end is always a thought away. Liberation—a simple choice. The way *is* easy and without effort. It rests in the *power to decide.*

We love you, and we are with you always. And we will never, ever, ever contract from any experience or thought you choose. For it is our delight to extend the good, the holy, and the beautiful. And can this be but Love being extended to God's Creation: you—*you!*—the Holy Son of God? Beautiful are you! Radiant are you! Innocent are you! Powerful are you! Eternal are you! Free are you! Loved are you! And we *cherish* you, now and forever!

Practice well, and enjoy your next thirty days.

Be you, therefore, at peace, beloved friends.

Amen.

Lesson Seven

Now, we begin.

And indeed, greetings unto you once again, beloved and holy Children of Light Divine. Once again, it is our *honor* to come forth and abide with you, to communicate with you in this manner and in this hour. We come forth, yet again, to join with you because the sole purpose of Creation is to extend the *good*, the *holy*, and the *beautiful*.

And what greater *good* could there be than to create a medium of communication that can call forth from the Christ Mind to every aspect of the Sonship in such a way that that mind is stirred to seek ways to heal its illusions and therefore return home to the recognition of what has never changed?

What could be more *holy* than to use each moment of relationship in the recognition that only God's Children can truly relate one to another, and that the purpose of their relationship is to heal illusion, that the *holy* might be extended?

And what could be more *beautiful* than to join together—you and we—in this moment, to recognize that what is truly *beautiful* is the recognition that *I and my Father are One*?

Therefore, the extension of the *good*, the *holy* and the *beautiful* needs to become *your sole purpose*—as it has become ours. For only when the mind is used for this purpose *alone* can there be the perfect remembrance of the Kingdom. And you have sought us out because you desire the Kingdom, because the weight of your illusions has become too painful. The games that you have sought to play within the dream of separation no longer satisfy, no longer seduce you, no longer gratify your imagination. And beneath all dreams, you have heard the call of the One who sent you forth, and asks you,

> *Little child, return! I am with you still.*

> *Let us create together the good, the holy, and the beautiful.*

The only difference that can yet *seem* to remain between us and yourself is that all of us involved in this work, from what you might perceive to be the "other side," are merely beings, aspects of Mind like yourself, that, within the illusion of time, within the playing out of time, *seem* to have chosen before you to heal all illusion and return home. Therefore, we call to you from across the very thin veil of illusions that yet seems to keep you where you are—seemingly separate from us.

That illusion, by the way, is not the physical body, nor is it the physical dimension, since in Reality, the physical dimension does not exist. What exists is *thought*, streaming forth from mind, creating, or outpicturing, that which has been held within the mind. So the very physical body becomes only a *symbol* of what the mind has decided to believe:

> *Surely, I am separate from God. That is the outpicturing I want. So I will look upon a physical body, identify myself with it, and therefore seem to peer out from the body and see great distance between*

myself and others. And if there is a great distance between myself and other bodies or forms, then surely there is an unfathomable gulf between myself and God.

But when perception has been cleansed, when perception has been purified, the body, itself, becomes *transparent* to consciousness, to the witnessing awareness of mind. And it sees no longer that with which it is identified. It sees only the phenomena of mental energy temporarily being played out in the field of space and time.

The body, itself, no longer becomes a barrier or obstacle to overcome. The body, itself, no longer is seen, or perceived, as something that can bring Love *to* it, or can reach out and attract or draw to itself what has been perceived as valuable in the world. Rather, the body becomes one thing: a temporary opportunity to extend the good, the holy, and the beautiful. In other words, even the body, itself, *can have no purpose*, save that which the Comforter, the Holy Spirit, the Right-mindedness within you, would give to the body.

Therefore, if you would know a body at peace, if you would know a body that serves only the function of being a communication device for the Love of God, cease in perceiving it *as your own,* and *give up* the apparent right to make decisions *for yourself*, in regard to the body.

We have suggested to you before that you cease using the term "my" or "mine" whenever you refer to the body. Merely refer to it as "*the* body"—as a carpenter would pick up a tool and say, "the hammer, the saw," or an artist would say, "the brush." For the wise carpenter does not identify himself with the hammer or saw, and the wise artist does not feel neglected when the brush is laying in a tray. Wisdom, then, looks upon form as merely temporary communication devices. The *delight* is to extend the good, the holy, and the beautiful.

Illusions can seem to take many forms, yet they all have one source: a *decision* to perceive oneself as separate from God. The best way to do that is to convince yourself that because you are separate from God, there must be many things about you and your life that are out of alignment with the Will of God. Therefore, you will manifest many variations that seem to express the instability which *is* the effect of that one belief, one perception:

> *I am separate from God. I have accomplished the impossible. Let me keep it in place.*

Illusions, then, while the form of them may seem to be many, are really one. And healing occurs when, in the depth of the mind, the decision is made to *surrender*, to give up the insane idea that one's self could possibly exist apart from the Mind of God.

Surrender means *to settle into the position of the servant*, the *conduit* through which the Mind of God, the Love of God, can be expressed. The mind that exists in perfect surrender sees absolutely no purpose to any moment of experience save this. The mind in perfect surrender looks out upon a world that has been healed from its own misperception that the world has had power over it. It sees that at no time has it experienced anything but its own outpicturing. This is why all events are neutral. It is *mind* that interprets an event, draws a conclusion, and then bases behavior upon it.

The mind that is healed, and that rests in surrender, looks out upon an innocent world that has been touched by *its* blessing of forgiveness. And that forgiveness is simply a step in which that mind recognizes that the world it had thought was there was nothing more than its own mental creation—and smiles and laughs and sees that the world has held no power, and that all events that have arisen, all *interpretation* of events, have been generated from within the kingdom of the mind—the one place that it is given unto you to assume responsibility for, as *your* domain.

The mind that has been healed of illusion has been healed of *all* illusions. And while time and space seem to last, the last outpicturing of a tiny, mad idea—called the physical body—can be given over to something else, can be transformed into a simple communication device that no longer communicates separation and judgment, but rather, forgiveness and innocence. It becomes nothing. And it is picked up and used only in those ways that can speak, gesture, move, act, make something in the world that touches the world with the blessing of the good, the holy, and the beautiful.

Because this is simply the Truth, it must mean that where you perceive justification for anything less than peace, it must mean that you have already decided, in the deeper part of your mind, to maintain this root, or core, misperception. That is, you are still attempting to perceive yourself as having accomplished the impossible—to have separated yourself from the Mind of God.

The mind that is surrendered looks out upon all things and quietly says within itself,

> *There has only been God. And I am the Created of That. And the source of my being, the source of my reality, rests in surrender into That, and That alone.*

The mind that is surrendered, yet walks in your world as long as the body lasts—and is often completely unrecognized by others around it, for others see a body and therefore assume there is an individual, an ego, a separated being within it as that body—you could say that body walks as an empty shell and is merely waiting to be *in*formed by the Love of God. And when the Love of God does not inform you or ask you to move and take action, then simply rest and do nothing. This is why the final state of awakening is incomprehensible in the languages of your world, since your languages are based on the very thought of separation, itself.

This is why, when we speak of peace, we speak of that peace which is *beyond all understanding*. For the peace that you can *understand* in the languages of your world are *conditional* peaces, the kind you create when two warring nations sit down with suits and ties on and forget the body counts and the destroyed villages. And they sign some document with a pen. They put on a "front" and smile for the pictures, and then they assume—and teach everybody else to assume—that now there is peace. Then each goes back and secretly continues to build weapons of defense against the attack sure to come from the one still perceived as an enemy.

Peace cannot be bargained for. It is not the result of compromise. Peace comes *only* when any mind surrenders *unconditionally* the dream of the dreamer him or herself, so that there is only God and God's creation. And we have shared with you before that that creation is one—the Christ Mind. And that Mind is not in body. It is not a particular form, and certainly does not belong to any personal entity. I was never "The Christ," as though you are not. Like you, I was a temporary modification of eternal energy, an outpicturing of a thought, a mental thought, held in mind, which learned to surrender the misperception of the dreamer, and became *in*formed only by Christ Mind. Only that Mind was present, and yet it could not be touched through the body. That is why my crucifixion had no effect on me, whatsoever. It merely sped up the process whereby the body was dissolved away as an idea.

Beloved friends, those of you that have been with us monthly, so consistently, come now in your understanding, as we take pause slightly from all of the technical work we've been doing of late, to change how you *use* consciousness. Take pause with us to remember the Truth: *The world that you look out upon is innocent.* The *cause* of the world is not *found* in the world, but only in the thoughts held within the mind. You remain perfectly free to choose to *perceive* differently. You remain free at all times to see that you are not the victim of circumstance, not the victim of a relationship, a career, what you call being born into a certain nation. You are never the victim of anything, since nothing within an illusion holds the power to truly have any effect on you. *You* are the one who remains free to assume responsibility for the domain of your mind. You are the one who is free to simply say,

Father, nevertheless, not my *will but* Thine *be done.*

And what will does the Father have, save that you be happy, by returning to the peace that forever passes all understanding? What could your Father will for you, but that you awaken from the dream that there is something *in* the world that can add value to you; that there is someone, some career, some location, some what-have-you that can actually *add* substance to your being? And better than this, to become freed of the perception that the *lack* of someone, something, some career, some location, some form of any kind, could *detract* from your being, from your perfect power of union with God.

Peace, then, comes from a decision, and then a decision that is put into practice over time, in which the world is *released*. And released from what? From your belief that *it* should somehow be for you the conduit whereby you *gain* good feelings, love, peace, wisdom, ideas, comradeship, and even brother- or sisterhood.

Detachment does not mean avoidance, but it does mean *dis-identification* with a mistaken idea. All suffering stems from this: identification of the deep mind, or the soul, with the forms that pass as outpicturings in this illusion . . . the belief that *loss* is possible and also that *gain* is possible. There can only be the recognition of what is true through the practice of extending the *good*, the *holy*, and the *beautiful*.

When the mind reaches this following point, the end of illusion is very, very near. When any mind looks out upon its creations, that it has attempted to make of itself, and finds all of it lacking—something missing, the life is simply not there—when that mind simply decides to withdraw the value it has placed on the world, and rests into the simple desire to be with God, then Heaven is but a step away.

And that final step is taken *by* your Creator *for* you.

The dream of separation has been your responsibility. When you reach that point of collapsing, so to speak, or surrendering, you enter into the stage of *restoration*, or *salvation*. And *that* is in the hands of your Creator. When restoration has been completed, and the mind no longer seeks to journey out into the fields of illusion, but simply rests, empty, at One with God, *then* creation can begin anew, and co-creation is in the hands of both you *and* your Creator. The only difference is that you are no longer a separate being, like a gnat shouting at the universe, demanding that things be done your way. But rather, you are empty.

You are the paradox of all paradoxes, for you are filled, and only Christ abides. And yet, not you lives, but only That One. And even the arising and the passing away of the body is of no concern for you. You merely rise in the morning and simply say,

Father, how would you have me be present this day?

And something else *in*forms your steps and your decisions. And you are no longer *identified* with the *fruit* of your action. You are no longer concerned with how it may look, or how it may compare to somebody else's action. You merely abide where you are, doing what you're doing, offering it freely, because you are no longer attached to it.

Peace is the essence of the message that we would share with you in this hour . . . again, as a temporary break, a temporary resting period, from the work that we've been doing this year. Rest assured, there is much more to be done. For when the mind is surrendered, resistance dies to the very extension of Creation. And that mind no longer seeks to leave any dimension whatsoever, for where would it go? It merely becomes one willing to enact whatever is being extended to it from the Mind of God, as a way of being involved with the extension of Love.

That requires, then, learning how to use consciousness differently. But it is all predicated on a return to peace. That is why, above *all* things, your responsibility is to enter into *surrender*—to let the tiny mad idea of a separate self be dissolved entirely from the mind, so that there is only the Mind of Christ.

Beloved friends, pause then, in this moment. Observe the place that you are. In Truth, is there anything around you in your current environment that could *add* anything to your substance? If you could find a way to possess it or digest it, would it puff you up? It might add a few pounds if you happen to have ice cream in front of you! But that is only to the body.

Likewise, as you look upon your environment, imagine if the things around you were taken away. Would that *take* anything *from* you? And if you can feel the simple Truth of the questions that we are asking, then surely you can come to sense that just beneath your involvement in the world of form, *peace is already available*, because Love waits on your welcome.

Will the world of form seek to pull you into identification with it? Oh, yes, because that is part of the very outpicturing you once created:

> *Would that I could create a world that will pull at me so much that it will distract me from the one thing I need to do. And when it does, I can say that, well, I'd be awake now, except that all of these other things, and all of these other people, need my attention more than God. And so, if only they would go away, I could know God. If I could just disappear into a cave somewhere, or a cell in a monastery, and shut out the world, then I could know God.*

That approach never works.

Recognition is not dependent on any specific state of body or lower mind. It is not necessary to spend endless hours in meditation seeking to quiet the mind. It is only necessary to withdraw value from what arises in the field of the lower mind, so that, quite naturally, what arises, what is recognized, is the *perfect value* that is held in *your prior union* with God. This is why awakening, salvation, or enlightenment, is not a change at all, merely a recognition of what has always been, what will always be—*eternally*.

Now—in this moment—are you free to choose anew. Now are you free to rescind your judgments of the world. Now—in this very moment of eternity—you can choose to recognize that you are *already* perfectly awake, freely choosing what outpicturings you will pour forth from the mind; freely choosing whether to think for yourself or to think with God, whether to believe your outpicturings, or to see them as temporary clouds passing through an infinite sky that the clouds have never affected or influenced. You are free now to simply say within yourself,

> *I can choose peace instead of this. I* am *surrendered, and nothing matters save the extension of the good, the holy, and the beautiful. Therefore, Father, in* this *moment what is Your Will for me?*

Empty of self, empty of striving, empty of the need to be right, the need to judge, the need to perceive anything in any certain way at all . . . Freed from attachment to the *fruit* of your action and yet, paradoxically, allowing creativity to flow through you, trusting that there is already a greater Mind that knows how best to serve the Atonement—the uplifting of the whole of the Sonship, every brother and every sister, who are but aspects of Mind . . . not *your* mind, for your mind is an aspect of Mind . . . points of light, seemingly fragmented from the One Mind, the One Light.

Free to see (and please listen carefully)—*right where you are*—free to see that the separation never occurred. And all attempts to keep it in place have been like battling for the rights of a chimera to exist; like insisting that the illusion of an oasis seen in a desert is truly real, and instead of going to the location and finding out what is real and what is false, standing there bickering with your arms folded across your chest arguing for the right to be right ... while Reality slips through your fingers. All the while, you're standing next to a beautiful spring which bubbles forth with the purest of waters. You are free now to entertain one idea totally insane to the world:

> *I am awake now. My dream has not occurred. No separation has occurred. No distance has been traveled. Grace has already restored me, and I am free to perceive the real world.*

We would ask, then, of you this: each of you who will be listening to this tape, to spend some time doing what we just suggested—to sit quietly and ask the questions that were asked just a few minutes ago about adding and subtracting from you, or to you. Sit with the words just uttered, over and over again, without being in a hurry, without struggling. And see if you can touch the place that knows the Truth of those words, so that that Truth is *felt* to be your own. Then, and only then, will you finally begin to dissolve the power that you have given to the ego. And what is the ego but the bundle of sensations and perceptions and outpicturings that are the very *attempt* to do the impossible, to be separate from God? Would you be willing to surrender that value, to rescind it, to bring it back to your heart and soul, and then offer it to your Creator?

Here, then, is the point of *conversion*, the turning about in the seat of the soul that must be reached by anyone who, in Truth, would seek God: to realize that they live, yet not themselves, but That One who extends power and Life has brought them into being. And they have a function to fulfill. It is *their* function and no one else's. And it cannot be compared. It can only be allowed.

Therefore, spend some time—as much as you want for the next few days of yours. And by the way, to those of you who feel that you are going to be "too busy," then let your time be used in busy-ness, and thereby, continue to try to convince yourself that the world is real. Wait for a few days, until you come to your weekend, perhaps. Then when your boss tells you you have "time off," *then* sit with the Truth.

For as this Truth settles into the soul, all that we have been doing prior to this will become easier and make much more sense. And it will clear the space for what is to come. For when the mind has truly awakened from illusion, there is nothing left but to be a servant of the Atonement. And the only question left is,

Father, how this day might I serve?

And with that, we'll bring this short message to a close. There is no need at this point for a continuation of words. There is only the need for *direct experience* held within the aloneness of your own mind and being. For revelation is *intensely personal*, and cannot be communicated to anyone at any time. Yet the revelation that comes to each mind may come in a unique way, but the revelation is of one Truth. That is why, when any two beings happen to meet each other who are awake, there is little to do but smile . . . and allow the phenomena of Life to continue.

Therefore, know that we love you greatly. And *we* honor *you* for the courage it takes to let go of the world and open the palms of the Heart to the Grace of Heaven.

And rest assured that when we continue in this series, there will be much to do. But let it be done from the perspective of delightful innocence, in a mind that recognizes there is nothing else to do with time except extend the *good*, the *holy*, and the *beautiful*.

We have paused, then, to remind you of peace. We have paused to remind you of the Truth. Offered to you, it yet remains to be seen whether the offering will be received.

Peace, then, be unto you always. And go in peace this day.

Amen.

Lesson Eight

Now, we begin.

And indeed, once again, greetings unto you, beloved and holy friends. We come forth to abide with you because you have asked. We come forth to abide with you because we are a part *of* you. We exist where you are. We abide as the Truth of what you are.

Therefore, beloved friends, please well understand that when we reach back into time, into the field of what you call *physicality* to create a communication medium with you, we do not come to you from some other *location*, we come forth unto you from the depth—the Heart, the Essence—of that which Mind is, that which Love is, that which Consciousness emerges from. We come forth from Reality. And we join with you in the only place that genuine communication can occur—*in Reality*.

This can only mean that in those moments when you *feel*—not merely intellectually consider—but when you *feel* yourself immediately and truly comprehending that which is communicated, or mediated by the words that we would choose, it means that, in that moment, you do not abide in time, you do not abide in illusion, you abide in Reality. And in *that* moment, there is, quite literally, *no distance* between us.

We speak here of distance, not just in what you would think of as physical terms, but there is also no distance between us *qualitatively*. That is, in that moment when you receive Truth, it is not the case that we are above you, beyond you, or have even gone ahead of you a little. You are comprehending the essence of Truth from the essence of Christ Mind, which is the *only* Mind that can comprehend the Truth and Reality of God.

That Truth is necessarily within you, and has been within you since before the birthing of time. It has been with you since before a tiny, mad idea seemed to creep across the expanse of your mind and you chose to believe it. That Reality cannot be taken from you. And it is *from* that Reality that you have awareness of your own existence. It is *from* that Reality that you gather the fuel, so to speak, to create the perceptions that you most desire. And the perceptions that you *most desire* are precisely the ones that you are experiencing *in any given moment*.

Now, to those of you that were abiding in Reality as you heard those words, you immediately know that that means that at no time and under any circumstances are your perceptions being, shall we say, thrown upon you from some source or force outside of you . . . that in each moment, you—and you alone—have created the perception, and therefore, the experience you are having within the field of the mind, for no other reason than that you have desired it.

This is why the very pathway of awakening, regardless of the form it takes, is *always* a *retraining* of the mind. It is a *decision* to choose to discipline the mind in each moment, to teach only Love, to hold only loving thoughts, to recognize that there is no such thing as an idle thought, since each thought or perception held in the mind *immediately* generates your experience. And that experience is like a pebble dropped into a pond that sends a reverberation, a vibration, throughout the field of your being. And that field goes far, far beyond what you commonly perceive to be the boundaries of your body.

Beloved friends, you will only experience what you desire. And that is why *desire* is always the first and most fundamental key to the process of awakening. It is why *desire* is the energy known *equally* by *all* minds, in *all* kingdoms, in *all* dimensions, in *all* worlds. It is by *desire* that you *choose* to relinquish the value you have placed upon limited perception. It is by *desire* that you decide to teach only Love. It is by *desire* that the Kingdom is restored to your mind. For it is by *desire* that you have been birthed from the Holy Mind of God.

The simplest way to discover what it is that you desire in any moment is to simply stop and observe,

> *What thoughts are currently taking place within my mind? How am I perceiving the world that seems to be around the body?*

And most especially,

> *How am I perceiving myself in this moment?*

And with honesty you will see quite quickly and quite easily what it is you have most desired to experience in this moment.

It can, indeed, be quite shocking when awareness begins to turn back on itself to *observe* the mechanics of its own thinking processes in the world, and then to hold the thought that the thoughts that are, indeed, dancing in the mind are there for no other reason than that they have been *desired* by the Truth of who you are. And you are that *power*—that *power*—which has been birthed from the Mind of God . . . made in God's image, that is, with infinite power, to create what you choose to experience. Desire, then, is integral to the understanding of the very process of transformation, for what you desire, you *do experience*.

When I walked upon your plane, your planet—which, by the way, does not exist independent of me even still, and exists *nowhere* save where you and I are joined as one—and that will give you something to think of . . . when I walked upon your planet as a man, seemingly cloaked in a body or as a body, I, too, had need of learning to observe the nature of my own mind, and to discover what it was I was desiring in any given moment.

Vigilance for the Kingdom means to retrain the mind until it desires *only* Love, *only* the Kingdom, *only* enlightenment, *only* peace, *only* Reality. And when the mind has been so retrained, in that moment there is no longer any sense of a separate self struggling to find God. There is no longer any sense of a separate self who knows lack. There is no longer any sense of a separate self that is unworthy of being the embodiment of Christ. And in that moment, the body can seem to continue or it could disintegrate.

And, at any rate, the body itself will be perceived in

a very different light. No longer seen as something dense and hard, that seems to separate you from your brothers or sisters, it is seen only as a dance of shadow that provides Christ an opportunity, temporarily, to speak the language of those that believe the body is yet real in order to communicate, to drop a pebble in the pond, that sends a reverberation, a vibration, through the body that is *emanated* and is recognized by everyone—perhaps not accepted, but recognized.

This is why you've heard many, many stories, some even related to me, that when a master, to use that term, walks upon the planet, something occurs in the energy field, the mind of those in his proximity—or her proximity. There is an energy that is transmitted. It is not that the master changes them; it is that the Truth in *them* is suddenly *quickened* into at least a very temporary *remembrance* of what is true. And an illusion can be dropped. Or perhaps, all illusions can be dropped.

The body becomes almost a magical means of communication. It appears to be something solid. It appears to be who you are. And yet, when the mind has been retrained thoroughly, and purification has been completed, the body simply becomes transparent and meaningless—except for the extension of the Light of Love.

Now, I have shared with you many times that to awaken as Christ requires that you *begin your journey as Christ*. It is not possible to transform yourself in order to *become* Christ, but it is possible to simply accept the idea of the Truth, and then let that be the foundation from which your life expresses itself. So that you begin to *think* with Christ. So that you begin to *breathe* with Christ. So that you begin to *envision* with Christ.

The Way of Transformation—and please listen carefully—is not a process of changing the unworthiness in you to the point where, *finally*, you're knocking at Heaven's door, and you then awaken. Rather, *The Way of Transformation* rests on your decision to accept the Truth that is true always:

> *I and my Father are One. Now that that's out of the way, how would a Christ live in this dimension? How would a Christ bring himself or herself to each moment of experience? What voice would Christ listen to? What vision would He serve?*

The *struggle* to awaken is the very *obstacle* to its accomplishment. And that is why the five minutes as Christ was given to you as a very simple exercise. And if, indeed, you desire Christ above all things, would you not participate in it each day? For that which you *desire* and *love* is that which pulls your attention to it. If you love Christ, then let Christ pull you, so to speak, attract you to spending five minutes a day in the realization that you can only be what you are created to be.

And having accepted that as the Truth, then inquire into your own Christ Mind on how you will live this day. For the mind that is awakened sees no distinction anymore between being here and not being here. It sees no distinction between Heaven and Earth. It sees no distinction between eternity and time. It sees no distinction between the non-material and material, or physicality. It sees no distinction between the extraordinary and the ordinary. But rather, Reality is returned to the mind, and it *suffuses* what the mind experiences.

And the literal world that you thought you used to know—buildings, cars, governments, and all the rest—simply becomes a temporary harmless illusion that seems to have "hoodwinked" (that is a very good term—hoodwinked) your brothers and sisters, who are a part of you.

And because the world is now seen in its transparency, it is no longer fearful to you. And you are *free* to walk and abide in it as long as the body lasts—quietly, joyfully, going about your most *extraordinary ordinary tasks*, except that they have become translated into the means whereby you demonstrate the Truth of Love to the world.

Reactivity, suffering, doubt, depression—in other words, dis-ease—can only be the reflection of a *decision* to use the power of the mind to desire, and therefore to perceive and experience, what is *unlike* the Truth of the Kingdom.

Freedom, peace, unlimitedness, and above all, fearlessness must necessarily be the result of the decision to use the power of the mind to remember, to realize, to abide in, and to extend the Truth that is true always. And then the passing phenomenon, called life, is simply seen as a delightful dance. It has no purpose in and of itself. Once, you gave it a purpose unlike God's. But as Christ, the purpose that you see in the world is *shared* by your Creator *with* you, and your will has become the same as God's: merely to abide and to be of service in the process whereby those that have been "hoodwinked" can remember the Truth and become free. And it no longer matters how that occurs, that is, what *form* your teaching occurs in. It's all the same. And you see no difference between your form and someone else's, for you will recognize the teachers of God.

And where you are in any moment becomes a *divine gift*, literally dropped in your lap as an opportunity to enjoy the *remembrance* that you are One with God—that everything you're seeing is a passing illusion, in the sense that it used to have a purpose that seemed concrete and that purpose has dissolved and gone:

> *Where did the world go? I used to think it was a fearful place. I used to think that I had to get ahead. I used to think that there were those who could victimize me. Now I just see harmlessness. I see nothing out there that can add anything to me. I am simply at rest and at peace, delighting at play in my Father's Kingdom. And where I am, Christ abides.*

So the distance from where you may yet perceive yourself to be and where you may perceive us to be is only the distance of a decision. That decision waits upon your welcome. And *no one* can take from you the *power* to decide to *own* your identity as God's Child.

Look well, then, in this moment. Stop and look within the mind. Then observe the simple day that you've been living thus far. And ask yourself what have you *desired* in this day? And allow memory to bring to you choices that you've made. Look upon those choices for whatever feelings, perceptions, thoughts you may have had. Look upon them with perfect innocence. Simply observe:

> *Oh, in that moment I was certainly not desiring peace. In that moment I certainly wasn't desiring perfect remembrance. Hmm . . . how interesting.*

And if you can find a moment in this day that you have lived so far—even if, by the way, you're listening to this tape five minutes after you get up out of bed—if you look well into those five minutes, you just might discover that there has been at least a moment in which you were not deliberately choosing to desire remembrance of union with God. Now, does that mean that you're walking around saying,

> *I desire union with God. I desire union with God . . . ?*

No. Those are just words. The *desire* is a *feeling*. It pervades the heart. You might say you feel it in the body, which is really just the depth of the mind, anyway.

Look well and see if there was a moment in which you were using the power of the mind to decide against the Kingdom. When you find that moment, just look at it, observe it with innocence, and simply say,

> *I could have chosen otherwise.*

And that is the simplicity and the power that the Kingdom is!

The world remains *uncaused* by *anything* outside of your own mind. Yet within it, you are given *complete dominion*. This means that within the One Mind of Christ, if you would perceive it for a moment as an ocean, individuation occurs; individual waves arise, made of the same substance—perfect freedom, perfect knowledge of, and union with, God. And in that freedom, the power to decide or to desire is present. And *desire* begets worlds without end. That is what your entire planet once came from. That is what your entire solar system came from. Your entire universe was born of desire.

The key, then, to the transformation of your lived experience, while the body lasts, is to *assume complete responsibility* for how you are choosing to use the mind. Remember you can only think a thought; you can only have an idea. That idea cannot enter your domain, over which you have complete dominion, unless *you* have sent it an invitation. That is simply the way it is. And it is a mirror of what God is—infinite and perfect freedom. That which I refer to as God simply never deviates from *desiring only* the extension of Love, the birthing of that which is like unto Himself—you. And your will is joined with your Creator's when you decide to birth only that which reflects Love—the *good*, the *holy*, and the *beautiful*.

The mind, as you've come to know it, will deceive you into thinking that,

> *Well, if I live that way 95 per cent of the time, then,*

*what the heck, 5 per cent of the time I can do
something else.*

And that's absolutely true. And yet, the more you
come to truly desire only that which reflects the
Truth of who you are, you will be able to tolerate less
and less variance within yourself.

This is why, when any mind truly begins to awaken,
it becomes more and more *painful* to continue
certain thoughts or behaviors that do not reflect
the deep desire of the heart. This is why the gap
becomes less and less—the gap of unconsciousness,
the gap in which the mind tries to defend its choices
and perceptions—until *finally*, it rests in *complete
vulnerability*. It lives in *complete innocence* and no
longer—and please listen carefully—*it no longer fears
change within its system of thought*. It no longer fears
being challenged by another mind, because it thirsts
only for the creation of a thought system that can
birth forth the *good,* the *holy,* and the *beautiful.*

It no longer explains. It no longer defends. It no
longer seeks to convince. It merely *abides* and gives
itself over to the stream of Love that would flow
through it. And every idea presented by another mind
becomes something to live with, something to digest,
to see if there is a jewel within it that can add to the
beauty of its own expression of the good, the holy,
and the beautiful. Everything becomes, what is called,
your "grist for the mill."

And there is no longer a need to be in defense. The
body does not tighten. The breath does not grow
short. There is only *vulnerability*. There is no longer

a need to hide. There is no longer the need to be concerned with the perceptions of others, since a perception cannot harm you. There is only *such love of self* that nothing less than God will do!

And so, again in this hour, we speak on the theme of *desire*.

And we seek to bring you to the point of realizing that *desire* is the great *power* of creativity. It is that which *births* your very experience. Desire is perfectly free. That desire, that power to desire, is within you and you will never be without it. It is *impossible* to be desire-less, since you can only find yourself to be where you have *desired* to be. Even if you are in deep and perfect silent meditation, you are there because of desire.

Therefore, beloved friends, please decide this day to take responsibility for what you desire. Recognize that *what* you desire will be what you *experience*. Recognize that what you *desire* literally creates the pathway whereby you will experience either Heaven or hell, peace or turbulence, Love or fear. And in each moment of desire, right where you are, you have just birthed an entire world. For out of that desire, you will create your perceptions of everything from yourself to the farthest of stars, all in a split second, a moment of timelessness.

Part of the journey, then, of *The Way of Transformation* is learning to transform your lived experience, so that you enjoy it more and more; are attached to it less and less; and fear it not at all. There are many in your world who would yet perceive spirituality as a way to *get out of* the place in which they find themselves, not understanding that they can be nowhere save than in their own mind. And as long as there is a desire to get out of where they are, they will remain stuck within it, because only Love can heal.

Therefore, the way of healing, which is *The Way of Transformation*, requires that you turn back to look at your creations, to look back into your own mind and to bring Love to whatever is arising, out of the *desire* to be the presence of Christ.

Now, does this mean that as long as the body lasts and you find yourself in the world of space-time and movement and all the rest—does this mean that you won't take the body from one location to another? Of course not! Does it mean that third-dimensional relationships won't come and go? Of course not! It *does* mean you become completely free of the old perception that an attraction to a certain relationship is going to add something *to* you, or the avoidance of a certain relationship is going to keep you safe. Rather, you begin to be free to let the dance of the third-dimensional illusion simply have its day. But it no longer holds power over you.

The highest state of awareness, then, in which perception has been totally cleansed and purified, is one of *paradox* as soon as you seek to talk about it. For you will look upon yourself and see yourself as a body-mind, with a certain name, living in a certain place on a certain planet, doing a certain thing. And in the *very same moment*, in the very same field of your mind, you will *know* that you are not that body, that you are not that name, that you are

not that history . . . that you are something more,
you are something grand, you are something divine,
you are something mysterious, you are something
beyond comprehension by any mind, at least in the
realm of thought.

And you will literally *know* and *feel* within the core of
your being the Truth of *both* of those. And there will
no longer be opposition between them. You will no
longer look at the personality and see a great schism
between it and the nature of Christ Mind, for the two
will have become merged as one. You will look at the
most ordinary events that you experience with your
body and see no differentiation whatsoever between
that and the Kingdom of Heaven. It simply is arising,
and is literally held in, pervaded by, and suffused by,
the *Reality* that is true always.

You will know that you are totally free when you no
longer feel any *obstruction* to whatever is arising in the
field of your experience. Why? Because you'll simply
see it as another opportunity to say:

> *Holy Spirit, what would you have me say? What
> would you have me do? What would it be like in this
> moment for me to simply realize that only Love is
> Real?*

And then, you will listen to that Voice. You'll feel it
deep in your heart. And you will simply act on that
Voice and none other. You won't listen to what other
minds think you *ought* to do. You will simply listen to
that one Voice. And it won't speak to you from the
ego, for *there will be no judgment*. And you will simply
come and go as one unknown by the world, and yet

one who looks to be very ordinary, one who looks to be the same as everyone else. The difference is that though the body still seems to walk upon the Earth, *you* are literally *embracing* the Earth. And in you, you will *know* that fear is gone.

Desire, then—the theme of this hour. And we would wish to extend to you some simple exercises that you can put into practice. We mentioned one of them already. A second is this: Take ten minutes out of each hour. Set your alarm on your little watches. And for ten minutes actually observe how you are moving the body:

> *Oh, I just got off of the couch and I'm proceeding to the kitchen. Why? Oh, I'm having the desire for ice cream. It has arisen as a thought in the mind and I have given it the power to motivate the movement of the body to take the action necessary to now put my hand on the handle of the refrigerator. (And by the way, I must say that I would have liked to have had one of those then). I am now opening the freezer and I'm taking out the cold little carton made out of the body of some tree at some point. And in it is a substance that some other mind created out of desire. And now I'm picking up a utensil, called a spoon, born of another mind that had a desire to make life easier. And I am dipping it into the ice cream, and now I am putting it into the body, which itself is the result of a desire. And I am creating my experience!*

And no other cause is there but this: the arising, the inception of a thought, a feeling, a desire which has birthed the entire movement of a world, called the body, to create an experience of eating ice cream. And you can do that for ten minutes, just by observing what you actually are doing.

Now, what does that mean? It doesn't mean,

> *Well, I'm going to work in order to pay the bills.*

No you're not.

You're going to work because you have held the desire to create something that seems to give you a semblance of safety, predictability and survival. "Job" or "career" is that which is birthed out of desire because of your perception of what you *think* you need. So you're not going to the job in order to do something. You're simply putting the body in the car and you are driving on your freeway.

Begin to learn how to observe without embellishment, without interpretation or explanation, exactly what you're doing—for ten minutes. Then if you want to go back to being unconscious, by all means do so.

But in this way you will begin to discern something that is also going on the whole time, like an underground current or river. For because you *are* Reality, there is *always* the desire to extend the good, the holy, and the beautiful. And by observing what you're actually doing, you'll discover that you're actually *succeeding* at that far more often than you give yourself credit for. You'll begin to see in some of your ordinary smiles, in the decision to take a card and send it to a friend, in the decision to refrain from a hurtful word—you will begin to discover that that, too, was birthed from *desire* within your holy mind.

And you will begin to taste that there is a *depth* to you that is already beyond fear, already beyond illusion, already resting in compassion and Love and wisdom and Truth. You'll begin to discover that you are already having many successes upon which you can build, many successes that you can acknowledge within yourself as a way of getting the taste, the feel, that,

Surely, Christ does dwell in this mind.

I once suggested to you that you remember only your loving thoughts. But the trick to that is that you must *first* become *aware* of them. So many become trapped in the depression and anxiety and insanity of the mind because they put all of their energy into perceiving what is *amiss* and no energy into perceiving their *success as Christ*.

So, in each ten minutes, learn to develop the ability to observe what you're *really* doing. And when you stop at your coffee shop on your way to your job, and you go in and you give some money to the person who gives you your cup of coffee, and you look them in the eye and you smile and say, "Thank you," you have just succeeded. You have communicated Truth. You have remembered that the one in front of you is worthy of your respect and Love. And *that* is a *success!*

Each time you can interrupt the momentum of the mind for perceiving nothing but problems, you'll begin to discover that the *underground river* of the

Mind of Christ is yet within you still. And as you *feel* your successes more and more deeply, that in turn builds your desire to live in that stream. And moment by moment, day by day, you will cultivate the power necessary to be identified with only *that* Mind.

And for a while, it will seem that there are two thought systems—the old one that you used to be identified with and the one that seems to be being birthed within you—you're really just remembering it. But *you* are choosing to bring the *discipline* necessary, the *vigilance* necessary, to retrain the mind to be identified—*not* with the realm of illusion but with the stream of Reality that is flowing through you, unimpeded, unobstructed, throughout all eternity, without end. Hmm . . .

That is the one gift time provides you. That's all there is. You can't use time to store up wealth in some bank account for the future, since the future does not exist, and you have no control over what will happen to your golden coins in your world. Time has only one purpose—the purpose the Comforter has given unto it. And that purpose is the Atonement of the Son of God.

Now, all of that sounds very lofty, and the mind goes,

> *Well, yes, of course. I understand that perfectly well, thank you. Good day!*

And then, that very mind goes right back to its same old patterns. Having heard, it has *not* heard. Having tasted, it has not swallowed.

Until you decide to *seize* time, recognizing its great gift to you—not as a punishment, not as a duty, but as an *opportunity* to become *wholly free*, and to smile within your heart because *you* know that you are One with God . . . to seize the opportunity to discipline the mind, so that it comes to be identified with the stream of Christ Mind, whispering like a quiet voice underneath the roar and din of the ego's conflicted world, filled with fear and doubt and judgment and the need to be right, the need to make others wrong, the need to believe that there's some power source outside of itself . . . when you awaken and realize that the Truth is true always, you will not ever complain about a moment of experience in which you have the power to desire differently.

For as you desire, you will perceive. And as you perceive, you will experience. And the whole game is simply this: *you're totally free*. Right here, and right now. You can't do anything to *become* free. You can only *remember* your freedom by how you choose to use the mind in any moment.

Time is an illusion. And the things that pass by, the phenomena of space and time, are just shadows that you have interpreted in a certain way. There is no gain; there is no loss. There is nothing to fear. The world can add nothing to you nor take anything away. You're merely here in this temporary classroom with an opportunity to do what any master in any dimension can do, for you hold the same power as I do—you hold the power to *teach only Love*. And what you teach, you must *necessarily* and *immediately* learn.

Therefore, learn well to observe the mind:

What am I really desiring?

Not,

What do I wish I were desiring? . . . What am I **really** *desiring?*

. . . remembering that everything is a neutral event. It's just a learning experience, that's all.

Separation does not exist. The Truth is true always. Death is unreal. You are Pure Spirit. Time is just a context. The world is harmless. You cannot be a victim. You are free. The Atonement is over. The ascension is completed. Once you get the message, hang up the telephone and get on with it by choosing to bring that Reality into the dance of shadow called "this world." For what good does it do to *pray* for freedom in the *future?* It is everything to *abide* in freedom *now!*

One last thing about desire. The egoic mind, which is made up of attraction/aversion, judgment, either acceptance or aversion, or hatred even,

This is right, that is wrong; this is good, that is bad . . .

Also be willing to embrace and accept the *results* of what you've been desiring. When you dip your spoon into your ice cream, enjoy it, *embrace it* as the effects of your desire.

And when you buy an automobile that breaks down, train yourself to embrace it and enjoy it, just like the ice cream. Why? For a very simple reason. If the egoic mind judges things as right or wrong, if you judge the ice cream as "good," but the breaking down of the car as "bad," *what mind* holds power over you? Are you free in that moment?

> *My car just broke down. Oh, but there's such a beautiful sunset! I think I might as well sit here and let the stars come out. After all, I really wasn't going anywhere anyway.*

Mind is everything. And if you *truly desire* more than *believing* in Christ, you must assume the responsibility for *transforming the mind* by using your very ordinary moments in which to see differently. And as you reshape how you use the mind, in every moment, you will come to taste profound freedom—a freedom that will carry you instantly far beyond the things of space and time. And they will seem to be arising within you and passing away within you: universes, arising and passing away, within the Holy Mind of Christ.

That is the great gift given unto you, then. And as we continue in this *Way of Transformation*, as you can see we've come around again to an old topic, called desire. What are you *worthy* of desiring the most? You will, indeed, discover and create your pathway to your own consummate awakening.

And, just to add one final thing, there can be no end to the Mind of God. You will abide forever within it, like one who abides in an infinite forest. Why not be *at play* in the Kingdom?

Enjoy your exercises! Some of you will actually

do them. And *those* are the ones who will taste a deepening remembrance of the Truth that is true always.

And so, be you, therefore, at peace. And again, we extend our thankfulness to you for having set aside the roar and din of the world to abide with us in this hour. For you see, communication is the great joy of the aspects of the Sonship who choose to come together to delight in remembering the Truth. Therefore, it is *our* delight to create communication devices to join with you. And you have a saying in your world, that "it takes two to tango." So, therefore, thank you for joining with us in this celebratory dance that remembers the Truth!

Go, then, in peace.

Amen.

Lesson Nine

Now, we begin.

It is not possible for you to be without Love.

It is not possible for you to be alone.

It is not possible for you to taste death.

It is not possible for you to taste genuine loss.

It is not possible for you to suffer the dream of separation.

It is not possible for you to be apart from your Creator.

It is not possible for you to fail.

It is not possible for you to harm anyone or anything.

It is not possible for you to be guilty of sin.

Beloved friends, as we abide together in this hour, please consider each of the statements that has just been made to you. We suggest to you that you pause the tape and write down each of them individually at the head of a piece of paper. Then once this session is ended, begin a process in which for one week you will abide with each of the statements just made. And what do we mean by that? We mean that as often as you choose, through desire, to set aside time to do so, merely abide with the statement. And then watch what comes up in the mind, and write it down.

What you will discover are many pictures, many ideas, even certain feelings that seem to indicate to you that the statement must not *entirely* be true. This is a way, then, for you to deepen your ability to observe what is actually occurring within the field of your own mind. It is a way to enter into a *deliberate purification*.

Denial can never purify the mind. For you cannot transcend what you refuse to embrace. For in embracing does Love return to the place where shadow once dwelt. And Love alone heals all things. The innocent need not fear. Therefore, because you are innocent, as you sit with this process, you are *completely free* to be *thoroughly honest* about what comes up into the mind as you sit with each statement.

Just jot it down. And after a two or three minute period, pause, look at what you've come up with, or what's come up within you, and then juxtapose those two views. Take the statement that you're working with and simply repeat it in the mind. And then look at the statement, the picture, the description, the memory that *seems* to indicate that your experience is *other* than that statement.

And as you juxtapose it in this way, look at what has come up within your mind—be *honest* about it—and then say . . . for instance, if it is an event that occurred last week, or last year, or ten years ago, or five hundred years ago (it doesn't really matter) as you look at it, simply ask:

> *Has this belief or this perception of myself, that seems to be in opposition to the statement on the top of the page, has it really changed anything about me? Has it taken my existence from me?*

And simply see what the answer is. Then lift your

eyes from the page and look around. And say within the mind,

> *I am free in this moment to choose to see things differently.*

Then take just a moment or two and abide—simply looking around you. Then go back to the statement at the top of the page and say it again out loud, at least three times. And then merely say within the mind, quietly,

> *This is the Truth about me. And I want* only *the Truth.*

And then, put it away, be about your business. At some other point, bring it out. And do that kind of process for one week for each of the statements given you. And rest assured, *purification* will be occurring in the depth of the mind. Each of you will experience it in your own way. But you will experience it. Remember always, then, that the only thing that can be transformed *is* the mind. And it is by the power of the mind itself that purification occurs.

Just as desire is essential to realization, so too is *willingness*, or *allowance*. And you have heard us say unto you many times that you are required only to offer a little willingness, just what you call in your world—what is this word—a "smidgen." Measure out a smidgen of willingness, which is the same as allowance, and sprinkle it upon your experiences. Sprinkle it across the world. Sprinkle it upon your own being.

Become willing to be one who cultivates the ability to *allow all things*. For the mind that is free can do this. The mind that is imprisoned cannot. For the mind that is imprisoned *is so* because it insists that what it perceives should become different *in itself*, but that the perceiver need not change. And that is the very essence of imprisonment.

One who cultivates that ability to *allow*, then, is cultivating, in Truth, the very act of forgiveness. It is releasing the *world* from its insistence that its perceptions be held as right. It is releasing from *itself* the need to *hold on* to its perceptions. Therefore, allow all things. Trust all the things. And thereby, embrace and transcend all things.

Allowance follows on the heels of desire. For when you desire the Kingdom above all things, you have no choice but to discover that you must allow the world to be as the world is. For you have not known how the world is—you have only known your perceptions of it. But the Comforter will heal those perceptions. And that requires your little willingness to let your perceptions be changed. And as they are changed, the world magically becomes a different place. It does become transparent and harmless. It becomes virtually *valueless*, except for the value that the Comforter would give it, while it lasts.

Allowance, beloved friends, is a process of letting go, is a process of trusting. It is a process of saying,

> *You know, I wonder what it would be like to just let things be as they are—to notice them and let them*

pass by?

Allowance is the doorway through which Christ passes into the complete remembrance of Christ. Allowance brings a deepening sense of freedom—freedom from all circumstance. For it is your circumstances that you have *believed* have the power to imprison you. But as you choose to relinquish your perception of the world, or any circumstance, you discover that you are already abiding in freedom. The *power*, and that is what freedom is, it is a *power* to create differently. And to create is the effect of what you will choose to see.

Allowance, then, can be thought of as a resistance being melted from the nervous system, if you will, which is just an aspect of the mind, anyway. Allowance is like the opening of the palms of the hands. Instead of holding on so tightly, you simply let go.

What do you let go of? The habit of the need to be right. The habit of the need to perceive that the world is a fearful place. The habit of perceiving that you are in lack. The habit of perceiving that Christ must be far from you. Anything that is unlike the Kingdom of Heaven is a habit well worth releasing by *allowing* it to be dissolved from your mind.

The essence, then, of this hour's communication with you is about the cultivation of allowance. It begins already, and will deepen a great deal, if you'll merely put the exercise that we began with into practice. The willingness to *relinquish the lid* you have placed upon your own mind, so that you become able, in innocence, to simply observe how it really is—what's really going on down in the basement, without judgment, without fear, without justification, without explanation. It is simply there.

In allowance, you cultivate the very quality of forgiveness. And without forgiveness, it is *impossible* to awaken into the realization of the Truth that is true always. And why? Because judgment is the opposite of the Kingdom. And where forgiveness is withheld, you are literally making a choice to be outside the Kingdom. You have used the power of the mind to make a decision, out of a desire to hold onto a perception, and thereby, you have generated direct experience. And *you* are the one who has kicked yourself out of the garden.

Remember, then, that always, forgiveness is *essential*. It is *necessary* for the Atonement. Forgiveness is another word for allowance. We speak here not of a blind passivity, but of a relinquishment within one's own mind, and that is all. It is a *willingness* to see the complete neutrality of all events. It is a *willingness* to let the Comforter remind you that separation does not exist, that you cannot possibly make yourself guilty of sin and all the rest.

Forgiveness is a *relinquishment* of what you have decided is true about the world. It is, then, very much a self-centered practice. Of yourself, you cannot forgive your brother or sister for anything, because, in reality, they've done nothing. Forgiveness is forgiveness of one's self for insisting on replacing Reality with your own version of it.

Allowance, beloved friends, is like the petals of a

flower, opening to embrace the new dawn of a spring day. Allowance is like the melting of the ice that allows the river to flow. Allowance is like the removing of a cap from a bottle of sweet fragrance and enjoying it as deeply as you can. *Allowance is the dissolution of fear. Allowance is transformation.*

And when you have come to allow all things, to trust all things, you will have embraced all things. And only that one who is *larger* than the thing which is embraced can do the embracing. Therefore, whenever you feel imprisoned, it is because you have made yourself *smaller* than the world you perceive.

And when you feel free, it is because you've remembered that you are the one from which all things have arisen. *You are* the Son of God. You are the vast sky in which all clouds and storms arise and pass away, while the sky remains unscathed—eternally changeless. *That* is freedom! And the cultivation of freedom is a free-will choice. It is the result of the *desire* for the Kingdom.

As you come *truly* to forgive yourself for every perception you have ever held about anyone or anything, you will come to discover that it means relinquishing perceptions of yourself, as well. For you cannot awaken fully unless you include *yourself* in the circle of your forgiveness. And ultimately, of course, you come to see that the very practice of allowance is *really* the act of *allowing yourself to be truly the Self that you are.* You will no longer *resist* the process of purification, by whatever means the Comforter uses for you. It simply doesn't matter any more:

Why resist it? All I want is God!

And if it is dissolved in the mind in a split second, and you don't even notice it—fine. And if it requires great tears and great experiences in the world—fine. What's the difference? They're really the same. It is because you have relinquished—through allowing—you've relinquished ownership of your own pathway home. And you have decided to let the Comforter *take* you home. Because you desire the Kingdom above all else, it no longer matters *how* that process is experienced. You no longer complain that it seems to be taking too long. You simply enjoin yourself in the process itself. You let the Comforter take you by the hand and retrace the steps you once made in error. And each step requires allowance, which is forgiveness born of desire that has been purified of desire for that which imprisons. And it is replaced with the desire for that which sets all things free.

Once your desire begins and becomes the Kingdom, the end of the journey is perfectly certain. School is out. That which the ego is cannot last. For the very universe, Creation, the world around you, will *conspire*—which simply means to *breathe together*—all things will conspire together under the hand of the Holy Spirit to create *precisely* what *you* require to be set completely free of all illusion. And secretly, you will have already agreed with the Comforter that it will be this way.

Allowance, then, is equally as important as desire, and is an aspect of that pathway, that foundation, whereby Christ remembers Christ and arises from the ego's ashes to walk upon this plane, and any plane, as the

Truth that is true always.

Remember that it is only the ego that will compare and contrast. It is only the egoic mind that thinks about another's path and wonders if perhaps their path is better than its own path, than your path. There is *only* the life that you are directly experiencing. And through desire and allowance, that very life comes to be embraced as the *very means* by which the Comforter is dissolving illusion from your mind. And of course, it's all based on the humility of realizing that the ego cannot awaken itself; that the Comforter *is* that agency, given by Grace, that knows how to bring you home.

I highly recommend that you establish a relationship with the Comforter as though it were a relationship with a good friend—indeed, the *best* of friends—until you reach a point in which virtually every decision is given to that Mind:

> *Well, old buddy, should I turn left or right?*

And you *relinquish* ownership of your life. It is only the ego that thinks it can possess life. Spirit knows that Life possesses it. That is, Life has birthed you; the Mind of God has given rise to you. You are God's. You are not the *owner* of Life. You are the *recipient* of it.

Would you then be willing, in this month's time, to make the decision to become a *grand master of allowance*? You can begin again with the simplest of things:

> *I allow this toothpaste to taste exactly the way it tastes,
> with no complaint. It just is as it is.*

If it is the changing of your seasons, would you be willing not to lament the end of your summer and the coming of your fall, but would you be willing to experience that change? For rest assured, and please listen well, in the realm of the world, which is the realm of perception, the *only* thing that exists is *constant change*. Underneath it there is a changeless Reality, that which pervades the changeable. But where there is resistance to change, rest assured, there is a mind living in delusion.

Remember that we have said unto you before that the Awakened Mind no longer feels any resistance to the things of time. It no longer tries to get rid of time. It no longer tries to make things stay the same. The Awakened Mind can embrace all things, trust all things, and thereby, transcends all things *instantly*, even in the midst of change.

In your realm—be perfectly honest with yourself—is there ever a moment in which change is not occurring? Can the body be the field of perfect silence? Hardly. Even if you make your heart stop beating for three seconds, there is still blood gently flowing through the veins. There are still thoughts arising, sounds coming in through the ears. The body is not that which can be changeless. The *awareness* of the body, the field in which the body arises, *is* changeless already.

Can you come, then, to be the *field of awareness* that can embrace all things which arise, change, and pass away, yet not feel any *obstruction* in embracing and dancing with those things? For the mind that is free from the illusions of death is that very mind that learns to *dance* with death, to enter into any moment or relationship, knowing that because the body is engaged, it *must* come to an end. In fact, it's already on its way to death.

The mind that becomes the one who is no longer in fear, no longer in resistance, is the mind that has forgiven all things, including itself. The mind, then, that can embrace all phenomena that arise and pass away with passion, with joy, with aliveness, with innocence, with simplicity—*that* mind cannot taste death. It literally transmutes death, even as death *seems* to be passing by.

The highest state of being, then, is always a paradox when you try to think about it. Through your *desire* you have come ever closer and ever deeper into the Kingdom. And through your cultivation of *allowance*, the Grace-filled willingness to know that that which arises is already passing away—it is like water flowing through a fork, and you might as well not lament it. The mind that laments it is the mind imprisoned in delusion. The mind that *allows* all things is the mind that is already freely *beyond* all things.

In this month, then, imagine that there has been given unto you a window, as though your Creator had plucked you out of Himself and said,

> *I'm going to drop you into the field of time because there's something I want you to learn. You now have thirty days in which to learn it.*

Imagine that if you didn't learn it, your existence would be snuffed out, what they call erasing your name from the Book of Life. Now of course, that will never happen. This is just a way of getting leverage on yourself.

Imagine that for the next thirty days all that mattered was the *cultivation of the grace of allowing*. How to do that? By coming down, once again, to the most concrete, most mundane, most ordinary experiences of any given day. When you turn your water on in your shower in the morning, to actually take the time to be present, and to feel its coolness change to heat and to recognize that you have just observed the constant dance of change in your world. And to say simply,

> *I allow this change to occur.*

Now, yes, it makes you sound that you're some great being, when in fact it's going to happen anyway. But have fun with it!

And if you burn your toast, take a deep breath. And before the egoic mind begins to complain and whine that its toast isn't the way it wants it, stop and look at it. Actually experience the burnt toast and say,

> *I allow this toast to be burnt. And now, I'm free to choose to eat it as it is, or to begin anew.*

If you get into your automobile, and you pull out of your garage, and the raindrops are hitting the windshield, simply give yourself permission to bring your mind back from the future into the present and say,

> *I allow the falling of the rain.*

That simple.

So, you see, the power of transformation of consciousness . . . which, by the way, is the only thing that can be transformed. Learning is a consciousness thing. It's the only thing that *can* be changed. It's the only place learning can occur. And all learning is designed to *translate perception*, so that it becomes more and more and more and more like Reality, itself. Fear dissolves from the mind. And then the Father can take the final step for you.

Learning *is* necessary in the field of perception. And *you* have placed *yourself* within that field. So, why not get on with it, and *let* perception be healed? It is healed by bringing the *power of observation* to what is right in front of you—not in front of the body, but right in the field of awareness, itself. And that is why you should be dancing in your shoes at all times:

> *My goodness, I don't have to go anywhere. It's right here in front of me. This ordinary moment provides the doorway to the transformation of consciousness itself. All I have to do is bring a little willingness to it. And guess what? I have all power under Heaven and Earth to do just that! Nobody can take it from me! Nobody can change the freedom in which I live! I am the one who can bring that little willingness to this moment and let the raindrops hit the window.*

If you will look around yourself, you will discover, in

any given day, plenty of things to keep you occupied, plenty of reasons why boredom is nothing more than a decision. For right in front of you is the richness of a pathway, translated by the Comforter, from a dream of separation to the royal highway to the Kingdom. And all power under Heaven and Earth lies within you—in *this* moment, and *this* moment, and *this* moment—to choose again. But it's time to take such statements out of the realm of abstract intellection into very concrete, if you will, *lived moments*:

> *Where can I choose again? Right now! I can accept and allow these raindrops to hit the window. I can be present with them. I can hear them. I can watch them as they trickle down, instead of being annoyed, instead of letting the mind go off into its future adventures. I can cultivate the art of being present now as the very presence of a mind that is free.*

Therefore, consider, in your days, in each of your next thirty days,

> *What could I utilize in this day to practice this exercise?*

Now, of course, that's a bit of an odd question to ask, since you can't be *without* things to put that practice into, practice with. It's impossible. Those that say they are bored are really saying,

> *I am resisting the Kingdom.*

Pure and simple.

Well do we perceive, once again, that so many in your world seek to find a spirituality that will free them of the world of their experience, never even realizing that *that very attitude* is the thing that chains them, imprisons them in their hell. Spirituality is merely a process of seeing things differently. And that is an *active decision*—born of desire, coupled with the little willingness called *allowance*—the decision to recognize that each moment is like a jewel presented on a golden plate to *you*, God's Child. You are the one who has the freedom always and literally creates, or makes, your experience. The final lesson that I had in time, concerning allowance, was the *crucifixion*. Now, I know that there are many of you that don't want to follow in my footsteps. But rest assured, beloved friends, if you would look well upon your experience, you've already tasted much more profound crucifixions *many, many* times. In fact, for some of you, my crucifixion was a *cake walk*, by comparison. You are free to crucify yourself no longer, by choosing to *transform* your very experience, by bringing the power of your mind to bear upon it.

Desire. Allowance.

So what, then, stands between you and the goal that you would seek? The *decision* to try to be *insane*. The *decision* to try to *resist God*. Now, you know that you can resist another body, since another body occupies another piece of space. In other words, it's not where you are, so you can resist it. But I say unto you, *God is already wholly present right where you are. How on earth can you resist what is already occupying the space in which you find yourself?* You might as well try to shake off your own hand, or shake and jiggle the skin off the body. Good luck!

All suffering is the resistance of Reality. All awakening and healing is the letting go of resistance. Forgiveness, allowance:

> *God is already here. And I am forever God's. I surrender.*

Surrender is the fruit of allowance. Surrender is the fruit of forgiveness. *Surrender is the same as the Atonement.*

But for now, simply focus on *allowance*, to make sure that you haven't left some dark corner in the mind filled with your need to perceive things in a certain way, your need to believe that the world should be other than the way it is, your forgetfulness that each event that transpires in your experience can be seen as Heaven or hell. As you choose to see only *Heaven*, you will discover the *power* that has already set you free.

The message of this hour is a short one, but it is quite long on value, if you will put it into practice. And after all, what else could you possibly want to use time for? You've tried everything else and found it lacking. You haven't been able to fill it up with enough lovers, enough money, enough cars, enough restaurants. Hmm ... So you might as well fill it up with the *transformation of consciousness*, so that perception begins to be more and more and more and more aligned with the real world. Why not? And if somebody asks you what you do with your time, say,

I grow Christ. What do you do?

So practice well! Begin with the statements given to you when we began. They're very, very important for you as a way of *triggering* the opportunity to observe what might be *unlike* the Truth still lingering in the mind. Some would say in the emotional field, which is really just the space of "glue" in which you attach perceptions, like pinning the tail to the donkey:

Stick that *one on the wall and keep it forever!*

Hmm! Let those things bubble up that they might be purified from your Holy Mind.

And above all, beloved friends, remember: *there are no mistakes!* You are free to trust the momentum that seems to be shaping your life. For you are the one who has complied with it by inviting the Holy Spirit to take you home. You are the one that has prayed for acceleration. Therefore, also be the one who accepts the Grace being offered unto you. Remember that resistance *is* the ego; embracing is of Christ. And the one that allows all things has already transcended all things.

Therefore, indeed, be at peace in this short hour. And let this hour become a month-long journey of exploration.

Be you, therefore, at peace this day.

Amen.

Lesson Ten

Now, we begin.

And indeed, once again, greetings unto you, beloved and holy friends. As always, we come forth in this hour with but one purpose: to join with the Mind of the Holy Son of God. For surely, this *is* what you are.

Beloved friends, we come forth to join with the Holy Son of God, to join with that Mind that was there in the beginning, before the mountains and seas arose, before the universe arose, before even the *thought* of space and time arose.

We come forth, then, to join with that Mind of the Holy Son of God that has remained in *perfect union* as the Sonship, in *perfect union* with its Creator, in *perfect union* with Reality, and with Love. And though we have said it unto you many times, we ask you to truly take pause and to consider this one statement: We come forth to join with you, *not* from a place above you or beyond you, but a place in which *you* already dwell, eternally.

No perception, no appearance can change the Truth that is true always. Even then, in this moment, as you hear these words, can you *feel* and *accept* the Truth of them? The only reason you hear them, the only reason you can sense the Truth that comes through them, is because you *are* that Truth, you *know* that Truth. There is, then, a place within you—unbounded, eternal, invisible, incomprehensible to the world mind, incomprehensible to the senses of the body, but perfectly and even simply comprehensible to the *silence* in which the soul dwells, comprehensible in a state of Perfect Knowledge.

All teaching, regardless of the form (and there are many forms of the universal curriculum), has but one specific goal: to nudge the mind of the dreamer beyond his or her dream, to return that mind to a state of Perfect Knowledge. Some would call it en*light*enment, that which suddenly is flooded with Light. And Light is Truth; and Truth is Knowledge; and Knowledge is Love.

Therefore, when we come forth in this manner to join with you, the only purpose that we have is to en*light*en you, to turn your awareness, to turn your attention to what you already know. And the only difference between knowledge and belief, which is the same as the difference between Love and fear (and that will give you something to think about) is that in a state of knowledge, in a state of en*light*enment, the resistance to the Truth vanishes—initially perhaps for just a moment, but eventually there is no longer any resistance to the simplicity of the Truth.

This transference, or transformation, from a state of fear to Love, or from ignorance (the ignoring of Truth) to enlightenment (the embracing and acknowledging of Truth) occurs for each mind within the dream in a very *specific* way. That is, it must occur according to what is required to release the patterns that have settled into that particular mind. In a general way those patterns are the same for everyone, but in their expression they take on a perfect uniqueness.

Therefore, the timing of your enlightenment, the

timing of your healing, the way in which it occurs, the contexts that are necessary for you to be challenged by your own self—so that that which is the belief you have been holding, born out of fear, can be brought to the attention and then released—will be uniquely your own. This is why, in *The Way of Transformation*, it is absolutely essential that you *never* compare your journey to another's By all means, yes, pay attention to the journeys of your brothers and sisters. Be open at all times—to learn, to grow, to assimilate, to apply, to integrate, to consider, to ponder.

The ego *always* compares and contrasts. It looks upon itself; it takes its self-picture and compares it to a picture of another mind, without even noticing that the picture is something *it* has created. It believes that it is seeing what is outside of itself, that the picture or the analysis of another actually exists in that other—and it may. The point here is that the ego compares and contrasts, and then draws a conclusion about its own worthiness, its own progress, its own state of illumination. All of this *must be* ego function, because, in reality, you are as you are created to be. And wherever you are in any given moment, enlightenment is but a decision away.

That decision entails but one thing: to release the insane valuation that you have placed upon everything and everyone, most especially yourself. That decision rests on the willingness to take God at God's word. That decision rests on your willingness to *cultivate silence*. The theme, then, of this hour is *the cultivation of that inner silence which is the threshold to wisdom divine*.

How, then, does the mind come to *true* silence? It is not merely, simply, a matter of closing the mouth. It is not merely, simply, a matter of shutting out the noise of the world. It is certainly not a matter of ceasing to listen to others, whether they speak the words of praise or words of criticism. Quite to the contrary. Silence can be cultivated in a number of ways. Initially, it will look like something you do through the body: to breathe deeply and rhythmically; to sit next to an ocean; to sit beneath a tree and become absorbed in the wind; to merely practice the ancient art of remaining silent, without speaking, as you go through your daily events.

All of these begin to cultivate a relaxation within what you call the brain and the body, the nervous system. Yet these things are merely projections of mind, anyway. So to still the body, to calm the body, to allow the activity in the brain hemispheres to relax and become more harmonious—this is, in fact, an initial step in bringing the mind to silence. But far deeper than these things is this: That genuine silence which is, indeed, the threshold to wisdom (and wisdom is nothing more than enlightenment) requires the cultivation of *deep self-honesty*. Honesty is that act in which *the mind is no longer committed to hiding from its own darkness.*

I have said many times, and in many ways, that it is necessary to enter into the blackness of the ego in order to discover what you want no longer. And, in Truth, for anyone who makes such a journey, that which the ego is becomes repulsive, repugnant, hurtful to one's self. And that is the only thing that matters.

Therefore, understand that in *The Way of Transformation*, although we've covered much territory in this brief year so far, a cornerstone of the universal curriculum must always be the cultivation of a *deep self-honesty*. And in self-honesty, one decides to simply *observe* the mind, itself, to simply observe the behavior that flows from the mind through the body, as it *gestures* itself out into the world. True self-honesty requires time. And why? Because the ego is the *attempt* to replace *honesty* and *Truth* with *dishonesty* and *falsity*.

Imagine, then, for a moment, that you are fully enlightened in this moment. You are abiding in a state of perfect freedom and peace. You are at One with God. Would there be anything that you would need to be dishonest with in your own mind? What corner of the mind would you have failed to embrace in Light? Therefore, in Truth, beloved friends, understand well that the ego is the attempt to replace honesty with dishonesty. It *is* dishonesty, itself. In fact, one could go so far as to say that those that would seek for the devil need look *only* at the ego—in which case the ego becomes *egocentric*, and your sense of identity is *all wrapped up* in defending and protecting a false image of yourself.

Much resistance is pervading your human domain, much energy of resistance, which is only this:

> *No, I will not look honestly. I must uphold the image I need to believe is true about myself.*

This is not Love and this is not Truth.

Beloved friends, take a moment, then, and simply cultivate deep self-honesty by merely answering these questions:

Have I ever had a murderous thought?

Have I ever manipulated another mind in order to try to gain what I believed I needed?

Have I ever withdrawn love for the subtle reason of causing hurt, or trying to cause hurt to another?

Have I ever had—shall we call them—disrespectful sexual fantasies?

Have I ever hated the world?

Have I ever despised myself?

And last, but surely not least, for in Truth, if you would consider it, all of those questions emanate out of this one:

Have I ever hated God?

Now, in perfect self-honesty, the answer to each of those questions can only be "Yes." And the honest mind looks upon all that has arisen within it without judgment. For there can be no honesty while there is judgment.

Think well upon the questions that we have asked you. And then simply take it a step further:

Has any of that type of thing within my mind occurred recently?

Notice what happens now. Pay attention to your mind and even into your body and breath. What occurs as you begin to get closer to the Truth? Do you notice a little bit of restlessness, the mind becoming more active with chatter? Decide for silence. Decide for peace. For healing occurs to the depth and degree of which the mind is willing to embrace what occurs within it.

Denial causes separation—self from Self, self from others, and self from God. And therefore, the very peace that the mind seeks through religious belief is impossible, as long as the mind is in denial about itself. Rest assured, when I walked upon your planet as a man, I, too, often became quite frustrated at the Pharisees who would stand on the corner in their long beautiful robes, *professing* religious belief. They had their just reward. And this is why I often said,

> *Beware of those who come in sheep's clothing but, inwardly, are ravenous wolves.*

For the dishonest mind is in conflict, constantly. It splits itself off from its sexuality as a human being. It splits itself off from its anger, its sadness, its hurt, its murderous thoughts.

But the mind that is healed has learned to turn and embrace every subtle shadow within the mind. For Love, alone, embraces all things, trusts all things, allows all things, and thereby, transcends all things, and need no longer live in fear that *those things* can run it. Enlightenment is a state in which the world—and the world is not outside of you; the world is the context, the thoughts and images and perceptions that you have attracted to yourself—the world can no longer hold power over you.

It doesn't mean that it ceases to exist, and this has been the great error of what you call religion as opposed to spirituality. Religion will give you a set of beliefs, ideas about yourself, standards that you must *achieve*. And thereby the mind concludes that,

> *If I'm to be a spiritual person, I cannot be angry. If I am a spiritual person, I don't have sexual fantasies about my neighbor,*

etcetera, etcetera.

And all of that is absolutely false. For in reality, the experience in your domain is one in which the mind has created and *is aware* of all things unlike Love. It then splits itself off and projects an image, called the ego, to itself first, and obviously to others, that it most wants to *believe* is true.

But remember, *belief* is not *knowledge*. Knowledge, alone, allows the mind to observe what arises within it without judgment, without fear, without identifying with it. It looks upon the world in perfect forgiveness:

> *Ah, I just had a murderous thought. I had a picture of hitting my employer over the head with a sledge hammer and watching the blood spurt through the broken skull. Ah yes, well, just another thought arising and passing away in this domain. It does not change the Truth of who I am. And I am free to extend Love or to hit him with a hammer.*

The mind which is free and at peace is no longer conflicted within itself. The mind which is unconflicted abides in perfect vulnerability. It has learned to embrace and accept the Truth about the phenomena of the mind itself, in this dream world. It is willing to begin to be honest and to cultivate deeper honesty with everyone around them. No longer is there pretense. No longer is there manipulation or control. There is no unconscious, split-off energy actually running the show, even though that mind seems to be oblivious to it.

The mind in conflict with itself is *dangerous* to itself, and of course, by extension, to everyone else in all dimensions. Therefore, indeed, beloved friends, beware of those that come in sheep's clothing but inwardly are ravenous wolves. *Beware of the viciousness of the ego within your own mind.* How does it come to you in sheep's clothing? Does it minimize hurtful behaviors? Does it minimize what is truly merely a lack of self-responsibility? Does it always make excuses why your life is not progressing in a way of becoming more and more empowered to bring forth Christ?

Learn to cultivate self-honesty. Though it sounds like a simple thing, this does take time, simply again, because the mind has used its own power to be *in denial* about its own miscreations. It doesn't want to own them. It doesn't want to embrace them. It wants very much for you and itself to believe that it's really a very high spiritual being. And it will wear the *sheep's clothing* of the ego, of the persona, the mask, the self-image, the projected image into the social world. And it will cling to that like a robe around the body, held against the cold winter wind; and it will cling to it, no matter what. Such a mind is an *insane* mind, and an insane mind is hurtful. An insane mind limits the flow of Love through it that could heal this world.

Therefore, beloved friends, as we begin to move toward the close of this year of transformation, we begin again to bring the arrow back pointing at ourselves, to point at the depth of the mind and to learn to observe it. If you take the list of questions that we have offered unto you and simply repeat that process on a daily basis . . . So, you see, we first began in the safety of allowing you to look way, way, way into the past, to see if any of that has been ever going on in the mind. Now we come closer and closer to the self-honesty of what is occurring in the mind anyway, right here and right now, so that each day you ask the same questions and see what the answer is.

In this way, the mind will become more and more transparent. You'll learn to look upon your murderous thoughts, all of those hideous, un-spiritual things that you have tried to shove down into the basement. And more and more, as you tell yourself the truth about them, the more and more you find a friend or two willing to tell the truth about their own minds with you—the more the mind becomes *transparent*, the less and less you have any need to hide. And a mind no longer committed to hiding becomes transparent to itself, and *through* it the Power of Christ can begin to move—with certainty, with knowledge, with grace, and with compassion.

The mind, then, has always been the problem—but not the entirety of the mind, just a small corner that's been fenced off, called the ego. When you became identified with only that part of the mind, you became *egocentric*, is your word. The center of your identity became the ego and *that* is the source of the problem. Quite frankly, it's like identifying with a pimple on the skin, and then defending the pus within it at all cost.

Silence is that doorway that will dissolve that pimple and that pus, forever. Silence is arrived at in many ways, but the principle cornerstone is *deep self-honesty*. The act of transformation, then—*The Way of Transformation*—is a process whereby you put the *squeeze* on the pimple of the ego and you no longer care what pus comes out, because you just want to be done with it.

Self-honesty *is* the *greatest act of Love* that you will ever experience within yourself—greater than any sexual union, greater than any adulation of the world, greater than any mystical experience. The embracing of deep self-honesty, the mastery of it, is the greatest act of Love that the mind can experience. For in *perfect self-honesty*, the world is transcended, fear is dissolved, enlightenment is present. And in enlightenment there is remembrance of perfect innocence, in union with God.

Therefore, indeed, beloved friends, you who would, in Truth, come to know Christ: look not outside yourself. For the Kingdom is within. The mind is your domain and the mind *is* your self. It has certain components: an emotional component, or expression; an egoic component, or expression. The ego, in itself, isn't right, wrong, good, bad; it simply is. The mistake—the knot in the rope, the blip on the screen—is merely the *mistaken identification* of your self *with* the ego.

That is what creates a tension, a twisting of the rope that ends up distorting everything. You end up being in judgment of yourself because you had a sexual thought yesterday—Heaven forbid! You judge yourself because you feel a little angry. You judge yourself because a thought goes through the mind,

What's the point in being on the planet?

As long as you are identifying with those thoughts, you're in trouble.

But when you see them as just an innocent flow, a temporary movement of energy through a vast domain called the mind, then you know that you are free. And you begin to taste the spaciousness and the silence that always is around the edges of everything that arises in the mind. You begin to become identified with that spaciousness, with that peace. And there, wisdom returns gently. You begin, again, to remember that you were created to create. And creation is extension, not projection. Extension is that which *floods*, or extends outward, the good, the holy, and the beautiful.

You no longer make justifications for not taking action to extend compassion to other minds in the world, but rather, you begin to wrap yourself around this world, around this planet, even around this universe. And you proclaim and know in the depth of your being that *you* are the Holy Son of God and you *will not* settle for less than Heaven on Earth! No longer do the problems seem so large or complex, because you abide in a state of Truth and Knowledge that is bigger than the world. For you *know* that, through you, God can do *anything*—if only you will direct your attention, open up the floodgates, and allow it to happen!

You begin to step in to the greatest place of power that there is. And this is truly what was meant, in even your Christian religion, that Christ returned to Heaven and sat at the right hand of the Father. Now, who sits at the right hand?—the chief of staff, so to speak, the one who makes it all happen. To sit at the right hand of God is to allow *your* mind to abide in right-mindedness. And in right-mindedness you see no separation between yourself and your brothers and sisters, which means you see no separation between yourself and the world.

Getting to Heaven is no longer an attraction; *bringing Heaven* to this world *is*. Bringing Light to darkness is all that matters. Constantly desiring to bring greater Light to your own darkness is the way in which you live, moment to moment, moment to moment—greater Light, greater Light, greater Light:

>*What do I need to let go of?*

>*How deep can my self-honesty go?*

>*How wide can my compassion for life spread?*

What actions am I actually taking in this world?

What am I defending?

What am I afraid of?

Am I willing to become so powerful a conduit for Christ that I take on responsibility for the Atonement and tell Jeshua to move aside?

For the mind in right-mindedness serves only the Voice for God. It no longer has any interest in defending the voice of egocentricity.

Therefore, beloved friends, for the next thirty days, practice *self-honesty*. Utilize the questions we have given you—each day. Also, merely sit down with a pad of paper and a pen and ask,

What thoughts have gone through my mind this day?

And if you want, you can draw a line through the paper, down the center, and on one side put loving thoughts, on the other side unloving thoughts—remember those are just your own judgments—and see what comes up.

In Truth and Reality, in the physical domain and dimension, no one is without unloving thoughts. Why? Because the mind is a vast space through which, you could think of it as, radio waves are passing constantly. Quite frankly, and we have spoken to you of this before: in the end you don't really know who is doing the thinking. You're only aware of a thought arising in the mind. The ego says,

I am this. I am not that. This thought must be mine.
That thought must be yours.

In Truth, you are all swimming in the same sea,
and there is merely *thought* arising and passing away.
You do have the power to discern and select which
thoughts will hold *value* for you, but it is impossible
to push away what you have decided to judge as
unspiritual thoughts. Can you imagine becoming so
free that when a murderous thought arises, it makes
you *laugh*, and you tell the *truth*?

Ah, when you reached across and you ate the potato
chip off my plate, I saw an image of taking a huge ax
and cutting off your hand and making you eat your
own fingers. Ha, what a thought!

For it is the embrace with perfect self-honesty that
returns the mind to *sanity*. It is the refusal to be
honest that creates the conflict and tension in the
mind that is called *insanity*. And insanity is a state in
which the mind is not at peace, and Christ cannot
enter therein.

Many of you have come from a tradition that you call
your Catholicism. And within it there is a practice
called confession. And this is really the idea of that
practice—although of course, it's been used to place
guilt . . . that's not the point. *Confession* means to
be *willing to be honest*. The priest was meant to be a
representation, merely a symbol, of God or Christ
Mind, so that you could sit in your little box—which
is really a symbol of going into your own internal
privacy, if you will, and telling the truth to your
Higher Self, to the Self that loves you anyway, to

the Mind that embraces all things and transcends all things.

Now, in Truth, that Mind will not tell you that you must go say 947,000 Hail Marys and sweep the streets of the city. It will merely say,

> *Beloved Child, you are forgiven already.*

For you have returned to sanity by merely confessing, to the deepest part of your Self, what has arisen and passed away within the lower mind, the mind associated with the body in the field of temporality—just like going to the depth of the Ocean, into the silence thereof, and saying,

> *Yes, I was just out there on the tip of the foam on the wave . . . a lot of chaos out there. Hmm . . . how about that . . . yes, yes.*

And the Ocean remains as it has always been.

Lack of honesty in self leads to lack of honesty in relationship. And lack of honesty in relationship creates the tension and appearance of separation and guilt, which is the very nemesis that the soul is seeking to overcome. Self-honesty, then—the return to perfect peace—requires, in the end, the *cultivation of vulnerability*, for,

> *In my perfect vulnerability, I find my perfect safety.*

The vulnerable are the *meek*, those who have returned to their own innocence and know that the opinions and judgments of others cannot harm them. They live, merely honest with themselves—without pretense, without image, no longer concerned with *that world*, the insane world. They become more and more a conduit through which the power and Love of God begins to work. And through them, other minds are reached. And unbeknownst to them, they become a living, walking (as long as the body lasts) conduit through which Grace is transferred to other minds. And in the presence of such a one, other minds *heal spontaneously*. Other minds are attracted to such a being, not because they are doing anything, not because *they* perceive themselves as great, but because they know that only God is great. And there is no longer a self they are trying to defend. And everything becomes merely a context in which they can be used by the Holy Spirit to bring about the Atonement. They walk in the world, *unknown* by the world, *unseen* by the world. They seem very ordinary. They merely do as Love asks them to do.

You *are* birthing Christ. Nothing can prevent it from occurring now. Merely trust each moment. Surrender into each moment. Embrace your commitment to Reality. Teach only Love to yourself . . . by loving that which you have hated and judged, by allowing yourself to *feel* and *to know* that which is passing through the mind and body anyway. Embrace it. See your ordinary humanness, not as an *obstruction* to peace, but as that through which peace can be *extended*.

And with that, now, beloved friends, we bring this brief hour to a close. Simple though the message has been, there is a great depth and treasure awaiting you, if you will put it into practice with *passion*, with even *zealousness*, with full commitment to your own Christedness, to see that *you are worthy* of the *deepest honesty* that you can reach—that you can confess, that you can live! For ultimately, *the deepest, honest Truth is:*

I and my Father are One! I am Christ Eternal!

Therefore, indeed, beloved friends, be you therefore at peace this day. Have fun with the exercises we have given you. And *know* how much you are loved!

Go, then, in peace.

Amen.

Lesson Eleven

Now, we begin.

And indeed, once again, greetings unto you, beloved and holy friends. Again, as always, we come forth to abide with you in this hour—*not* from a place apart from where you are, but from that place in which the Sonship is joined as one. And where can that be, but in the Mind of God? And Who is God, but Love?

Therefore, in each moment, when any mind surrenders its identification with its illusions, when it surrenders its identification with its own thoughts, with its own needs, with its own perceived desires, and rests into perfect silence, it rests *into* the Voice for Love. And it learns to ask only of *that* Voice,

What would You have me do in this moment?

And, more and more, the Voice for Love begins to *in*form the decisions, the thought processes, the vision, the revelation—and in your world—the action or behavior that is expressed through the temporary coalescing of energy into the *illusion* of a body.

Therefore, indeed, beloved friends, we come forth from that place which *is* the Voice for Love. And if any mind can, indeed, rest into that place, it can only be because that place is *necessarily* within it. It is the depth of the soul. That depth is not an individual. It is universal, it is eternal, it is forever present. It knows no boundaries. It knows no time. It simply *is* Love.

So, we abide *in that place* and we speak forth *from that place*. And if you would well receive it, then, at any time, when anything uttered through this mechanical device you call your tape, through yet another mechanical device called, in your world, the channeling—when you, in your mind, are struck by the profundity, or the Truth, of what is being uttered—it is only because you have chosen *in that moment* to open your *own* internal access to the Voice for Love. And what is triggered, or what is activated, what is remembered, is that part of you that *is* Love Itself; that part of the Self, the depth of the soul, that is forever One with God.

The great trick of *evolution*, if you would permit me to use such a term, is *to grow the soul's awareness* so that it rests in that depth of silence, and yet does not need to withdraw or turn away from the expressions of creation to do so. That is, it need no longer judge the body. It need no longer judge the world that you see around the body. It need no longer strive to ascend to some spiritual height in which all things disappear. But rather, to the contrary, the soul in its *maturity*, if you will, has ascended into union with the Voice for God. That is, it has ascended into the depth of its Self. It has learned to stabilize Itself in that internal silence. And it has, through time, experienced that process of transformation in which even the conscious mind is no longer thinking for itself, but is *in*formed from the depth of the True Self, the depth of the soul, the Voice for Love, God Itself, Christ Itself.

Beloved friends, *The Way of Transformation*, then, involves the deliberate decision to allow the translation of perception so that it becomes of one mind, of one accord, with the Mind of God. It is *in*formed from the depth of the silence and Love that sees the body, that sees the world, that sees each moment *only as* that which holds the value which the Holy Spirit has placed upon it.

And what is the Holy Spirit but that part of your own right-mindedness that *knows* that only Love is Real. And yet, when any mind truly rests in that silence, it knows that it can no longer draw conclusions about what Love would do, what Love would express through it, how Love would use the particular tools or gifts of any seemingly individual self—in order to trigger, in order to nudge, in order to uplift, in order to *shock* any other aspect of the Sonship into desiring its *own* awakening.

Now, if you pay close attention to what was just said, the implication is perfectly clear. Reality is One and unshakable, and only Love is Real. Yet the dream should never be denied. For denial creates separation. Only embracing can allow healing, the healing that Love brings. Therefore, there are, indeed, as you well know, many minds that are still afflicted, if you will, still harboring the decision to believe that the dream of separation is real.

When any mind within the Sonship chooses to awaken and heal its own illusions, Love begins to inform that mind more, and more, and more, so that its expressions serve the Voice for Love. And the Voice for Love has only one purpose: to be extended *into* the dream, *into* the illusion, to nudge the aspects of the Sonship yet sleeping, that the *entirety* of the Sonship can be returned, or reawakened, to the Reality of Itself *as* the creative conduit through which God extends Himself.

When any mind, then, truly awakens, it no longer sees specialness in the world at all. Each moment is merely sacrificed, or surrendered, into what I once called *the Will of my Father.* And what is that Will?—*the impetus of Love.* How can Love operate so that it brings awakening to the minds involved? That is, indeed, *a purely creative process,* and is the only *true* value time can have.

The Awakened Mind, then, has no idea, one day to the next, what Love will ask it to do, how Love is to be expressed through it. The Awakened Mind knows that it is not the maker or the doer, and merely asks in every moment,

> *What would you have me do?*

And the more that practice is developed, the mind is refined and purified so that it becomes almost a spontaneous or second-nature kind of thing, in which the mind is so closely aligned with the Will of God that the subtle nudges, flowing forth from the depth of the Self, from the depth of Love Itself, stirs through the conscious mind and meets no obstruction born of fear. For where fear has been de-valued, Love springs forth.

And yet, such a one—and each and every one of you that has chosen to listen to these tapes has already made the decision to become *that one,* ever more deeply and ever more deeply; make no mistake about it, the decision has already been made and therefore the end is perfectly certain—when that mind, that has made the decision to allow its transformation, when that mind embraces the simplicity of its lived experience, it looks as though it is very ordinary. While the body lasts, you do the things that all bodies and minds do in your dimension and world. You perhaps find the body shivering against the winter cold, or sweating in the summer sun.

And yet, in the midst of the *contexts* of the experiences of your life, what is informing the mind are not the egoic desires of:

How can I get more?

How can I avoid a certain experience or feeling?

How can I make myself comfortable?

How can I get others' approval?

How can I be acknowledged as a great master?

. . . and all of the rest. None of that runs that Awakened Mind.

Each context, then, is surrendered within the mind, itself, over into the Will of Love. And that mind, through the personality, through the body structure, while the body lasts, becomes a *conduit* that serves the Voice for Love. And that one may not be understood; that one may not be approved of; that one may not be acknowledged by the world. Yet, rest assured, those who seek to be approved of and acknowledged by the world have their reward.

And what reward is it to be acknowledged by the insane, dwelling in illusion? Can an illusion truly acknowledge the worthiness of the Son of God? But to such a mind (and once again, each and every one of you is in an inevitable journey now)—you, too, shall have your reward. For there are those of us who know you and love you, and your acknowledgment comes not even from us, though perhaps through us, but it comes from That One that has birthed you to extend the *good*, the *holy*, and the *beautiful*.

The Way of Transformation, then, is not the *gaining* of power, it is the *release* of all illusion. It is the willingness to release the grip that you have had upon the shadows that your mind has made up as a substitute for the Truth of your *only* reality. The process then, of *The Way of Transformation*, is that process in which you begin to use the mind, quite deliberately, in a different way.

To some of you who have studied my *Course in Miracles*, that, too, is an expression, or a form of *The Way of Transformation*, since all transformation inevitably requires correction, *of how the mind is used,* so that what the mind *sees* is different than the ego's world. When the mind is corrected, the *use* of the body that most serves Love also naturally follows. The use of what you have created in error—which, by the way, is the body, the personality structures, the emotional matrix, the beliefs—all of that that makes up what you call 'yourself,' all of these things are given over to be used differently.

Therefore, the deeper you come to understand, to *know* and to *feel* the depth of the self that you have constructed, in your attempt to conform to an insane world, the greater the space there is for you to be *in*formed by Love. Not that the body disappears, not that the personality structures disappear, but rather they become *transparent*. The value you have given them has been withdrawn, and they are given over to be used in a different way.

To use a simple example, a painter begins to paint devotional paintings out of her love and acceptance of Grace. A speaker is brought into alignment with Love, and that Love creates a context in which what is spoken is spoken differently, with a different purpose and a different intent and, therefore, to a much different audience. One who works with the hands in the fields begins to work for a different purpose, begins to be informed in ways to use the skills and gifts that one has developed, perhaps to feed the hungry, the needy.

The forms of expression change to be more conformed with which *voice* is running the show. When the ego was running the show—or thought that it was—the personality, the emotions, and the body were used to serve the salvation, if you will, the very survival, of the ego. When the ego has been displaced and the Voice of Love, has been returned to the place of authority, careers can change, *for the very meaning and purpose of existence has changed*.

In the initial stages, as this process is occurring, this can, indeed, elicit fear, a sense of disorientation, a sense of self-doubt. All of these things must be embraced with faith, and faith is, indeed, the substance of things unseen. Love isn't quite settled in perfectly yet, and the mind is still gripping, somewhat, the things and the ways of the world. And yet, a deeper Voice is compelling the self to release old values, to release old careers, old relationships, old clothing, old furniture. Everything begins to change. And it feels as though loss is being experienced.

And yet, what is *loss* in the world is *gain* in the Kingdom. For what can be gained but the reawakening to the simplicity of the Truth:

> *I am God's. I belong not to the world. I and my Father are One. Well, since I still find myself in this world, how can I dedicate this bag of dust and its attendant personality and emotions to the Voice for Love?*

And that becomes the *sole purpose*—we could say both the only, as *sole,* and the *soul,* as the essence of your being—the sole purpose becomes the willingness to allow Love to *in*form each moment.

It is quite true that such a one, born of Love, can be very misunderstood by the world. Such a one, I once said, is one borne like the wind. You don't know where they've been, you don't know where they're going, and neither do they. But they are present where they are, constantly dedicated to being merely a servant of, or a conduit of, the Voice for Love—recognizing that time and the world no longer holds any function, value, or purpose, save that which the Holy Spirit would give it. And the only value the Holy Spirit gives the world is to see it as a *context* through which the Sonship can be healed and awakened.

The Way of Transformation does, indeed, require what
you may call commitment, what you may call a
deliberate choice. This can be the value, by the way,
of initiatory experiences. And, not too far in the
distant future, we will be helping to *in*form Shanti
Christo, so that initiatory experiences are offered and
provided. The value of this is that it makes conscious
and public what the soul is desiring anyway, and calls
the conscious mind to step into a *deeper self-discipline*,
a *deeper self-commitment*, a *deeper self-maturity*.

Indeed, beloved friends, *The Way of Transformation*—as
you have been playing with this process this past
several months of yours—is not something ever to
enter into in what would be called a *lazy* way. We
would highly suggest, then, that as you go through
the mind, ask yourself,

> *Are there any of the monthly tapes that I listened to,
> but with only half an ear, with part of my attention on
> trying to get dinner ready, or getting my taxes paid, or
> getting to the office?*

If there is any such tape that you have not brought
the *wholeness* of your being to, in a state of openness
and surrender, go back, and listen to it again. You will
discover that, lo and behold, there is much that has
been missed. Each exercise has been carefully chosen.
Each exercise offers you an immediate way to begin
to transform certain aspects of your own mind.
Therefore, *each moment* should be treasured.

And, please hear this: As the mind, the conscious
mind, begins to become more *in*formed by the Voice
for Love, vigilance and discipline become *even more*

necessary, simply because you're dealing with more power—more *true power.* The purpose of your very being takes on a far different flavor. And you begin to realize that wherever you are, there is a *precious moment* that offers an opportunity for healing, for Love, for awakening. And it is not to be missed. *Each moment* of your existence in this plane, this density, *is not to be missed!* Once, when this, my beloved brother, proclaimed to me,

> *Could you please come a little later in the morning? I would like to get some sleep,*

(at that time, three o'clock was about the appropriate time for me to reach out to him), my answer to him was then what I will give to you now:

> *Have you not been sleeping long enough?*

Will you use time constructively to realize that where you are is not in the world at all, but in a context made *new* by your desire to awaken, which invited the Holy Spirit to 'take over the show,' so to speak? And that wherever you find yourself is *not* an ordinary moment any longer. Though you seem to walk in the world, though you seem to deal with the things of the world—which you must do as long as the body lasts—you no longer *belong* to the world. Another Voice has touched you. And though your neighbors and friends, perhaps even your children, or your spouse, or your parents, cannot possibly yet see who walks among them, you are a *Disciple of Christ.* And Christ is the Father's only Creation, created in Love, as Love, to extend Love.

And you are in the most important journey that anyone can ever take—a journey without distance to a goal that has never changed, even into a place that is unchangeable forever. You have undertaken the journey from illusion to Reality, from fear to Love, from *false* power through manipulation, through image, through conforming to the world, to *true power*, resting in the Mind of Christ, being a *conduit* for that which awakens the Sonship.

Every function, then, is *equal* to those that have chosen such discipleship. Understand, then, that wherever you are right now, as you listen to these words—*wherever you are right now*—you are in the perfect place at the perfect moment. Therefore, indeed, bless the moment as you find it, for it serves two purposes. One, it is that perfect context for your awakening from illusion. And at the very same moment, it is offering you the opportunity to cultivate your skill at being a conduit for the Voice for Love. Two sides of one coin, existing *fully* in the presence of each of your 'ordinary' moments.

And rest assured, as you come to trust the Voice for Love, as one born of the Spirit, as one who lives as the wind, if it is time for you to release certain forms—career, relationship, clothing, furniture, what-have-you—[snaps fingers] you'll know it in an instant. You simply *know*! For revelation is knowledge. Knowledge is *immediate*. It is not translated through a whole lot of thinking in the mind. That is why we choose to say that it is through the *heart* that one knows the *immediate will* of Love.

And as you practice letting go of that which you once valued, you'll discover that it gets easier and easier, as with each experience of letting go you find yourself carried, in ways that you could never comprehend or create yourself, into new formats, new contexts, in which your own wisdom awakens even deeper. And the opportunity to be of service expands and grows, as though you stepped from a small room in a house into a larger ballroom and realized,

This is much *better than where I was before!*

It is not that you have failed when something ends. For, in Truth, you cannot fail. For, in Truth, there are no endings, *except* in illusions.

We speak, then, of what we will talk much about in the next month's tape—the importance and distinction of *content* and *form*. We will look at those two sides of the coin, and help to illuminate your mind and understanding that it is *content* that always matters, and that *form* is secondary. Form is what is birthed in *time*. And what is birthed in time, ends in time. Even the body had a beginning and will, therefore, have an end. And yet, when it is given over to the Voice for Love, its purpose becomes *timeless*, *endless*, for it begins to express *only content*. But again, more about that later.

In *this* hour, the theme that we would wish to bring unto you is this: *Make a decision*—right now—*to view time differently*. Put on the Eyes of the Holy Spirit—right where you are, *right now*. Don't just listen to what is said, but actually decide to do it. Look around the place you find yourself in, the body. If you are with others at this time, notice them. Notice all things. You are not in the world at all. You are a *Disciple of Christ*. You have chosen, by Grace, to awaken from illusion, and to cultivate yourself, with support and help, into being ever more a *mature soul* that radiates the Light and Love of Christ, even while in time.

Time, then, must be *seized* and seen to be of *great value;* that each and every moment is not a mistake. There is nothing "idle" about it. And you are the one who is free to use that moment to be *in*formed by the Voice for Love, to learn ever more deeply to surrender the value of fear, safety, personal survival, and all of the rest; and to dissolve, through faith, into the Voice for Love.

From *this* moment, decide to *see time differently*, to *seize the opportunity* to train the mind to be *vigilant* and *aware*. There is much occurring that may yet seem unseen to you—too subtle to grasp. You call it, 'being unaware.' But the journey from unawareness to awareness begins with the decision to walk through each moment of the day *knowing* the Truth of who you are—to embrace the purpose and reason for your being, and then to ask the Holy Spirit to make all things known and clear, in alignment with the Voice for Love.

The body becomes something that you no longer possess. The thoughts that you hold become meaningless. The context of every moment is *given over* to something new. And the decision to see time *differently* leads you into the cultivation of a way of *being* that is different and new. And eventually, it will move from a mere intellectual idea into something known in the depth of the soul and expressed through every pore of the skin, while the body lasts:

> *I am the Christ. There is only That One, and I am dissolved in and as That One. Call me not great, for only God is worthy of awe. That which I do, I do not of myself, but the Father does these things through me. I am One who merely loves Love* so deeply *that I am willing to surrender all things that I once knew to be my self, that my* true Self, *who is Christ, informs my every decision, my every gesture, my every extension of the* good, *the* holy, *and the* beautiful.

A certain phraseology that we are aware of in your language of your world is,

> *Hmm! This is some* heavy stuff!

It is *very heavy* to the ego, since it squashes it like a gnat under a weight. If the light of the sun, if the sun itself were to come and rest upon your planet, what would happen to your planet? It is much like that when the Light of Christ comes to descend again, to touch the mind and the emotions and the body—where once the ego held sway. The ego dissolves into Light Itself. It becomes remade, if you will. And while the body-mind lasts, it becomes a mere servant.

The mind, itself, laughs at itself a great deal. For it sees the great joke that it has played on itself. It attempted to be other than what God created it to be. And it experienced a multitude of dramas and illusions and story lines, careers, relationships, diseases, and all of the rest, in a *grand attempt* to be other than what

Reality is. And so, the mind that is awakening laughs at itself a lot. It laughs as the echo of old patterns show up. It tells the Truth about them. It need no longer deny them, for it holds no value, and the old patterns are not seen as a cave in which to hide. The personality becomes *transparent*. And in its innocence, it becomes perfectly *vulnerable*. And in its perfect vulnerability, it finds its *transcendent safety*.

Indeed, then, beloved friends, many of you began this journey out of curiosity. And yet, I say unto you, that was only the conscious mind's attempt to maintain control of the journey itself. But no one comes to these messages who has not made the decision from the depth of the soul,

> *I am tired of suffering. I am tired of aloneness. I desire to dissolve into Christ Mind and to discover the Truth of who I am.*

Everyone hearing these words has made that decision. And you're already well on your way. And if you think you can turn around and go back to the platform and cash in your ticket, forget it! The train has already left the station, the conductor is God Himself, and those that enter herein cannot leave. The ego will try to convince you you should, because it is fighting for its life. But there is another Who fights for your *true* Life, even that Comforter given unto everyone in the moment the dream began.

So, well do I know what *must emerge*, once the decision has been made. Each and every one of you will then perceive that your journey is unique and wholly yours. But this is only because you still perceive yourself as a separate being. Why? Because the eyes of the body show you that you are. Because you have lived with a certain husband, and you, therefore, know that everyone else on the planet did not. You will believe that that portion of your journey was "uniquely" yours—with "unique" energies that probably no one else could understand.

And yet, that was only the matrix, or the *form*, which was expressing a *content* of energy. And that *content of energy*—whether it be fear, whether it be jealousy, anger, whatever it is—*is known by everyone*. This is what we mean when we say there are no private thoughts, no private experiences. The body, of course, has its unique experience. Only one body can be in a point of space at any given time. And if you're making love in the middle of the night and you look around, you'd swear nobody else is present. Rest assured, you live in glass houses. And all things are perfectly visible to the entirety of Creation.

It is the *energies* that you are experiencing that everyone knows. And the trick of healing and awakening is to come to see the *neutrality* of all energy, so that you can choose to inform it with the value that the Holy Spirit would give it. Then, time becomes *sacred*. It becomes *eternal*. It becomes a *tool for Love*. Even the body becomes a tool that Love uses to bring about healing. What other purpose could a body hope to have?

So, indeed, please do the exercise of making sure that there has not been a tape that you have listened to with half a mind. Go back. If you wish, practice your five minutes as Christ, and then begin the listening of the tape—that your *soul* might *absorb* it. And when there are exercises to do, do them—even if it just takes a minute. You cannot begin to see how the pebble dropped into the pond can have such vast, vast and deep effects.

If you would still choose to look upon me as one who did great things, rest assured, the effects that you came to know about, because certain stories were told about me and then finally written down—and, by the way, some of those are a bit outlandish—those things came about because I, too, had teachers that showed me how to drop new pebbles in the pond of my mind, whose commitment and intent was the same as ours, which is to guide you into the fullness of your discipleship, until the transformation has been thoroughly completed on Earth—that is, in the body-mind—as it is already in Heaven. For the correction has already occurred. It happened the moment [snaps fingers] you had the thought of separation, long before space and time was birthed. But you discover that the correction has, indeed, been fulfilled as you *allow* your creations in time—the body-mind—to be transformed, so that the conscious mind becomes perfectly aligned with what the depth of the Self already knows. And then, and only then, can the mind truly release the illusion of the third-dimensional plane, the physical dimension. For it is simply seen as a useless limitation.

So in ending, then, this hour's message, do this one thing. In each of your next seven days, as often as you remember to do so—and remember, you will only remember what you choose to value—as often as you remember, *decide to see time differently* and *to acknowledge that you are a Disciple of the Mind of Christ*, and nothing matters to you than the simplicity of allowing the dissolution of illusions so that Christ can come and live where once the ego dwelt in authority.

A simple exercise. And if a day goes by in which you forget, it can only be because, in that day, you have valued something else.

And with that, then, beloved friends, as we prepare this hour's message, we would behold, then, that there is one who has some questions to ask. And they are both timely and important questions. We will, then, what you call the "shifting of the gears," before we bid you "adieu" is the word, I believe.

And so, then—questions.

Lesson Twelve

Now, we begin.

And indeed, once again, greetings unto you, beloved and holy friends. As always, I come forth to join with you, not from a place that is apart from where you are, but from that place in which we are eternally joined as one Mind and one Heart, one Truth, one Creation . . . one Love. I come forth, then, to abide with you from the place in which you dwell eternally. I come forth to abide with you because *I love you.* I come forth to abide with you because you are as I am—*the Thought of Love in form.*

And to those of you that have joined with us these many months of your year, we come now to the conclusion of *The Way of Transformation;* that Way, then, which allows the perception of the mind to be transformed from illusion to Reality, from fear to Love. *That Way* is the way in which you come to the brink, or to the edge, of the Kingdom of Heaven, in which you are *finally* ready to use the power of the mind to declare *only* what is true. And what is true is unshakable forever.

And at no time has a single illusion that has stolen across the vast expanse of your being ever changed the Truth that is true always. And the declaration of that Truth is the essence of words that I, too, once had need of speaking:

> *I and my Father are One. I, as a ray of Light, am One with that Source of Light from which all things spring forth. I, as a drop of water, am One with the Ocean from which all moisture arises. I am that One sent*

221

forth from Divine Mystery to bring forth the good, the holy, and the beautiful—to reflect in time, to reflect in form, that which is timeless, that which is formless, that which I have referred to as Abba, or Father, that Creative Source that births all things and has an immediate and direct relationship with all of Creation.

That Truth is true about you. It has been, in fact, the only thing that has *ever* been true. And in each moment, the power of the mind allows it to remember the Truth, if it will *choose* the Truth.

The Way of Transformation, then, has been designed to guide you with specific exercises, with many fundamental questions, to the brink of that decision in which the mind declares, for itself, from within itself, and then extending outward:

I and my Father, I and my Creative Source, I and Love are One. And from this moment forward, I walk and live as one who chooses to use the power of mind, the power of awareness, the power of intention, the power of clarity, the power of beingness itself, to know the Truth that sets all things free, to be the Truth that allows freedom to be extended to all others, to walk upon this plane, while yet the body lasts for a little while, as that One who has been sent forth as a ray of Light to shine Light into a world that has feared it.

I invite you, then, as we come to the close of this year's lessons, to truly set aside time to withdraw yourself from the roar and the din of the world, to withdraw yourself from all the beliefs you have held about yourself or about anyone. And there, in the silence of your own heart, to simply acknowledge that *the Truth must be true always*, and that *the time is at hand* for you to use the power of the mind given unto you of your Creator in the only way that it can be used sanely:

I and my Father, I and my creative Source, are One!

Why is this important? In the end, all technique, all methodologies and strategies, are really magical means for taking away the egoic part of the mind's insistence upon the authority of its illusions, to seduce, to trick the mind, to bring it to a place where it *must* come unto, in order to truly step forward—in and as Life, Itself. All strategies and all methodologies, even those that we've given unto you this year, are given unto you because the mind has been held sway by illusion.

The art of *lessening the value* that the mind places upon illusion is all that can be taught. But all teaching is designed to return the mind to the brink of the Kingdom of Heaven. There, and there alone, the mind itself, that which you essentially are, must, from the *depth of its beingness*—unattached to anyone or anything—the mind itself must declare its decision to be awake, to assume the mantle of responsibility for bringing forth into this world only the Light of Truth—in each moment, with each breath, with every gesture, with every intention, with every vision and thought, with every choice.

Indeed, beloved friends, *The Way of Transformation* brings you to the brink of *The Way of Certain Knowledge*. *The Way of Transformation* is a journey without distance to a goal that has never changed. It is merely a *change of mind*: the decision to value the Truth, and the Truth alone.

When that decision has fully been embraced—you might think of it as a full embrace that embodies every cell of your being, the totality of all that you are—it becomes perfectly devoted to your union with God, and the recognition that as the *Created*, it is time to relent, or repent, or to *surrender resistance to Truth*, and to accept that the Love of God has been given to you *fully*, without measure, without condition, and that you have been created to live *from* that Love . . . that *that* Love might inform every thought and every deed . . . that *that* Love might pour forth through you as the very Source of your own identity.

No longer I, but Thine,

would be one way of saying it.

When the mind has fully come to the recognition that no other decision holds value or purpose, that no other decision can bring the soul the peace and the fulfillment that it has sought in so many ways in the fields of illusion, *then, the Father takes the final step for you.* That is, by an act of Grace, that tiny drop of water that seemed to be so separate from the Ocean, dissolves and melts into the Ocean, Itself. And there is no longer a separate self to be found. The body-mind? . . . Yes, of course. It arises and continues for yet a little while, until its purpose is fulfilled. And then, it is put aside as a toy that has been outgrown.

The mind, the power of consciousness, slips into the perfect and eternal Truth that has been true always:

There is only the Love of God. And I am only in existence to express that Truth.

In *The Way of Perfect Knowledge*, all efforting is suspended. And the mind flows, borne by Love. It flows like the wind, knowing not where it comes from or where it's going, for its cares are not in the world. Its *certainty* is in Love. And peace pervades the entirety of the mind, wherever it *happens* to find its attention placed. And all things of the world have been translated into merely devices whereby the Truth might be communicated to the whole of Creation, to a brother or to a sister. For in Truth, all of you are exactly *that*—perfectly equal, perfectly innocent, perfectly radiant and shining, forever.

You become *The Anointed*. You become *The Messiah*, that which brings forth the Word of God, to use that language. You become *The Christ*. Yet, this is not an accomplishment. It is merely the return to an ancient remembrance of what has always been. The mind, having surrendered all resistance to Love, merely abides in the certainty of a *perfect* knowledge. This, then, awaits you *now*, on just the other side of a final decision.

Look well, then, at all that has transpired for you in this past year. Has it been by accident? Have the chance encounters, have the insights, the visions—has all of this been by chance? Hardly, for in the *depth* of your *being* you *chose* to enter into *The Way of Transformation*. You *chose* to open the depth of your being to a

225

reflection of the Truth you already know, given to you by an ancient brother who has loved you since before time is, one who has merely chosen to enact the extension of Love in whatever way is available.

As I have said unto you many times, I am not limited in how I communicate with any mind that would open a place for me. This context through which I speak with you now is but one of many. Yet it is the way in which many of you have made the decision to *allow* that communication to be known to your conscious mind. It is the context you have chosen to allow your release from fear and your embrace of Love.

I once said unto you that all things that begin in time, end in time, for their purpose is not to become a substitute for what is eternal, but to be devices whereby the remembrance of the eternal is returned to every mind which is a part of the Sonship—the One Mind, the Mind of Christ, in which you dwell and have your true being.

The Way of Transformation, then, had a beginning and it has an end. *The Way of Certain Knowledge*, which will comprise the whole of this next year's sharing, will have a beginning and will have an end. And rest assured, I say unto you, that when *The Way of Knowledge* has been imparted to you, and we have come into the perfect blending in which *you know* that you walk the plane as awake as I ever did, then the purpose of our three year teaching-learning period will have come to a conclusion.

This does not mean that I will depart from where you are. But it does mean that you will have stepped into the certainty that you are that One. And what you would seek to gain from me, you will find in the temple of your own heart. There I will join with you—not as your teacher or savior, but as your friend and equal, as a co-creator. You will be free then, because you will no longer be *seeking* knowledge from me—you will be *extending Love* from the soul of your own beingness. And you will be free to invite me as a friend to join with you in your creations. And that is an invitation that I will *gladly* accept! For the only purpose of creation is to extend Love.

Relationship is eternal. Friendship is eternal. Co-creativity is the *essence* of knowing God . . . co-creativity with the sole purpose of *birthing in Light* the *good*, the *holy*, and the *beautiful!*—that which brings the vibration of Truth and reflects it in the world of time; that which touches fear and dissolves it; that which touches guilt and replaces it with forgiveness; that which touches resistance and tension and replaces it with willingness and peace.

Can there be any purpose in existence but this? For this were you birthed in the Holy Mind of your Creator. For this have you journeyed through the labyrinths of everything *unlike* Love, that you might truly *choose* to return with perfect freedom into the *marriage* of Creator and Created; Divine Son, Divine Spark. For the union of Father and Son, or Creator and Created, is *so intimate* and *so perfect* and *so filled* with the *Perfection of Love* that, in Truth, you will look and see no longer where you end and the Father begins. You will be like the *perfect lover* of God, given over to that Love, pervaded by that Love, melting with that Love.

And yet, you will know always that you are the Created. You are like the Wave to the Ocean, and the Sunbeam to the Sun. And you will marvel with every breath. And spaciousness will come to the mind, and even into the cells of the body, in which you abide in the knowingness—beyond all conceptualization, beyond the reach of all beliefs, beyond the hope of every religion—the Reality of the Living Spirit of the Living God.

The Way of Transformation, then, comes to a conclusion as you sit quietly with yourself and look upon the past year's lessons, the insights, the changes, the chance encounters, and you *accept* and *know* that the being—the mind, the perceptions that began twelve months ago—*that being no longer exists,* except as the echo of an ancient memory. And *you* no longer need to invest the power of your identity with what is passed away.

The Way of Certain Knowledge begins with this. Rest assured, then, that in the next roughly thirty-day period, between the time that you receive these words and the time that new words are given, with a focus and a context which will be known as *The Way of Knowing*, these next thirty days are your *final transition*, if you will but accept it—in which you can turn away from the past and look back upon it no longer; in which you can step into the Light of the future of your own personal destiny, held in the hands of a perfectly loving Creator that *already* has a plan for you, or you would not have been birthed, for you are *certainly* not an accident!

This next thirty days is the *most critical* for you. For *it is now up to you, alone,* to decide to acknowledge the Truth, to decide what you are committed unto: the Voice of the Holy Spirit or the voice of fear. Are you committed to using the things of space and time to reaffirm the *old beliefs* that you are separate from God? Or will you use the things of time—allow the Holy Spirit to use them for you—to demonstrate for you that you are *in* the world but no longer *of* the world? You are no longer possessed and owned by the world, but you are *owned* by that Voice for Love that has birthed you and sent you forth to bring forth the *Word*.

And the *Word* is just that vibration in which peace, forgiveness, *knowing* abides. The Word is like a vibration, a wave that emanates from the depth of the Ocean, that speaks of the *good*, the *holy*, and the *beautiful*; that looks upon the things of space and time even upon the body—and sees *nothing* to be feared, but sees all things in their *perfect, harmless innocence*; that owns and embraces the totality of your perfect freedom.

You are Pure Spirit. You are as the wind. You can neither possess nor be possessed, for you are owned of the Creator. Love *embraces* you. Love *pervades* you. And you hear no other voice but the Voice for Love. And through your eyes will shine a light so clear—for indeed, the eyes are the window of the soul—through you can begin to emanate the Truth that is true always. And you will not fear looking into the eyes of a brother or a sister and saying unto them:

> *I am that One sent forth of the Father. And if I am with you in this moment, my only purpose is to be present as* Love—*with you, for you, for us, and for all of the Sonship.*

> *This is the choice I make. This is the beingness I bring. This is the Truth that I am devoted to. I bring you only Love.*

Indeed then, beloved friends, *The Way of the Heart* was designed to open you to the reality that within you lies a center of peace, a center of forgiveness, a center that can begin to take you toward certain knowing. *The Way of Transformation* was designed quite specifically—for those of you that truly enjoined it—to dissolve certain patterns in the mind, to reactivate your power to *deliberately decide* what you will think, what you will feel, what you will create, what you will believe, what frequencies of thought will be acceptable unto you.

And now, you come to the brink of a decision that *closes the door* on a past once made in error that has been corrected, through the Grace, through the gift, of the Holy Spirit and placed within your mind and heart—and the *opening of a door* of a Life lived not *seeking* the Kingdom, but a life lived *in* the Kingdom, *in the Light of the Kingdom of Perfect Truth*:

> *I AND MY FATHER ARE ONE. Nothing can arise by accident. And my only purpose is to embrace Creation, that the good, the holy, and the* beautiful *might be extended through even this body-mind,*

wherever it happens to be. For my delight is the Love of my Creator, my devotion to the extension of Love, my peace from the embrace of my brothers and sisters in the simplicity of a celebration that shall know no end.

I am perfectly aware that there are many of you, as you will be listening to these words, who will feel, yet, a subtle contraction, as fear *attempts*—one final time—to claim ownership of your being. You are free to choose otherwise. You are free to say:

No! It is Truth I accept. It is Truth I will know. It is Truth I will live—not for another, but for myself. For my only responsibility, from the moment of my creation, was to accept the Atonement for myself, to allow the transformation to occur in the depth of my own mind, so that ancient words become, in Truth, mine: I and my Father are One, and I know it! *Henceforth, I am free to walk this Earth in gentleness, not to strive to move into the future, but to be borne by the Wings of Love . . . to be borne by the Wings of Love that will carry me into the fulfillment of my destiny. And my destiny can only be that which reflects God in this world.*

Let not fear claim authority over the mind any longer. This does not mean that you won't occasionally feel it like a wave through you. The difference is that you *need not value it.*

The final stage, *The Way of Certain Knowing*, is to *claim your right* to be *perfectly happy*. And perfect happiness can come only from the soul's decision to acknowledge the *decision to value the Truth and to live it.* Nothing else can bring the soul to the completion of its peace. No other decision, no other thinking process, brings the Son to the Father, brings the Daughter to the Mother, brings the Created to the Creator, brings the Sunbeam to the Sun, brings the Wave to the Ocean—in perfect remembrance that *only Love is Real.* And what is Real cannot be threatened.

The world no longer holds the illusory power that you once gave unto it. It becomes no longer something you must conform yourself *to* in order to survive. For you are Life Eternal, and your Life is held in the abundance of God's Love. You stand, then, on the brink of the complete transformation of the perception of the world. It will be radically changed [snap fingers] in the twinkling of an eye as you look out upon it and say:

> *There is nothing here that has a greater power than the Love of God. And because I abide in that Love, I am freed from needing anything of the world. And I am free only to give to the world. And what I give is added unto me, for by teaching I learn, and by giving I receive. And my love of God is matched only by my love of My Self as that which God has created—perfect and whole and innocent. And my love for My Self is so deep and so purified of the falseness of guilt and smallness and egoism that I want all of God! And I will bring forth only that which allows me to feel and to know my Oneness with That Frequency and That Light.*

I once said that if you are not wholly joyous, it can only be because you have elected to use the power of your mind to think *differently* than your Creator. *The Way of Knowing* will bring you into the certainty of a perfect joy that is *unshakable.* Imagine, then, no more swings of depression, no more swings of self-doubt—just *pure beingness of Love,* right where the ego used to claim property rights.

The Life which you were created to live is in the palm of your hand. The decision to end this year of *The Way of Transformation* by simply acknowledging that,

> *Only the Truth can be true and I am fully committed to being only that,*

brings you into the Kingdom—no longer a journey *to* it, but now, the *eternal* journey *within it* . . . mystery upon mystery, miracle upon miracle, sublime beauty upon sublime beauty . . . peace, peace, growing into peace as you *surrender* and sink into the Reality of God's presence . . . forevermore, forevermore and forevermore. For God is without end and knows neither height nor depth. There is *no limit* to the Reality of the Creator.

And there can be no greater joy than to allow your consciousness, which is the gift of your awareness, to be ever permeated deeper and deeper and deeper by the certainty of a perfect knowing:

> *I AM THAT ONE! And I abide in that Love prior to every breath, every thought, every gesture. This body is not what I am, but I will use it as a communication device. I will not use it to separate myself from my brother or sister. I will use it to gesture in the ways of*

Love, the ways of respect, the ways of gentleness, the ways of embrace, the ways of appreciation, the ways of thankfulness. I will see my Father in my brother and my sister. *And I will love that and honor them as the vehicle, the conduit, that brings the Light of my Father to even my physical eyes.*

I will revel in the delight of how the sunlight sparkles on the dew upon the petal of a flower. I will listen to the barking of a dog and know that Mystery has been made manifest. I will walk this Earth as one who is free, and one who is the spaciousness through which only Love abides and is offered.

And many will be sent unto you who will awaken in your presence—in even 'ordinary' moments. *You stand at the brink of all that the soul has desired!* Is it not time to wrap the fingers of the hand around what has been placed in the palm?

I am that One.

Time to live *in* the Kingdom, guided *only* by the Voice for Love, by the Voice for Truth, by the Purity of Spirit.

So, I would ask you then, now, to set aside yet a little time in which you abide wholly with yourself. Acknowledge the Truth that is true always. I invite you to use the power of the clarity of your mind to decide *against* valuing illusions, and use that power to *value only the Truth*, that you might offer yourself *into* a Life through which the Truth that is true always becomes *concretely embedded in the totality of your being*. For you, indeed, will *know* the Truth and you will know that it has set you free.

Spend some little time, then, by yourself—quietly, *alone*. A long time ago, I said once unto you that the decision was made *alone, in the depth of your being*, to see if you could create *unlike* God, if you could transform yourself into something which is other than what God has created. That has been the whole drama and dream of the realm of separation. You *must* come back to claiming ownership, *alone*, in which you decide to use the power of the mind to make a *different* decision—in the *depth of your being*. For you stand *alone* before your God, Who waits patiently for His Child to awaken, to receive the gifts that the Father would bestow upon the Son, that the Sun would shine forth upon the Sunbeam, that the Ocean would give unto the Wave . . . all power under Heaven and Earth to bring forth the good, the holy, and the beautiful . . . to walk *in time* as one who is *timeless* . . . to abide as a body-mind, yet one who knows they are Pure Spirit, shining forth *temporarily* through the body.

It is given unto you, then—*now*—in the depth of your internal silence, *to reclaim ownership of your mind,* to let parents, to let society, to let everyone off the hook. No one has *caused* you to feel what you feel, to think what you think, to act as you have acted. You have used the power of the mind to attempt the great impossibility of making yourself into something that is *other* than what God has created. And now it is time to *deliberately* use the *power* of the mind to decide *with* your Creator.

The Way of Transformation

It is the end of all seeking. It is the end of all striving. It far transcends the purest and greatest of strategies and methodologies. It is beyond prayer. It is beyond meditation. *It is the simplicity of the Truth.*

Therefore, abide quietly. And for those of you that will, indeed, make the decision and will step across the edge, across the veil into the Kingdom, we indeed will abide together for yet one more year in *The Way of Knowing*—*The Way of Perfect Knowing*. And you will see the totality of your life *radically transformed*. For that *must* be the case when the *seeker* is no more, and it has been replaced by one who has *found*—and *acknowledges* it!

Miracles will lead the way. For the mind that is given to true devotion to the Holy Spirit is unlimited forever in all ways. And the whole of Creation shapes Itself to be of service to the One that is anointed and claims it, and lives only to give God to the world. Not one concern will arise before you that will not be taken care of and met before you run into it. The walls will dissolve.

You will be the miracle-minded. You will be the One who shines forth in perfect effortlessness, in perfect peace, and perfect joy. You will be Christ Incarnate. And that—*that*—is the purpose for which you were birthed in the Mind of God. And it is in That Mind that you are held—now and forevermore!

Be you, therefore, at peace—this day and always.

Be you, therefore, in the Perfect Knowledge that I am your brother and friend, and nothing but this. I am

That One who loves you and sees only the Light of Truth in you, and looks forward to the day in which we create together as *equals*, in honor and devotion to the Great Mystery that the Love of the Creator *Is*.

Peace, then, be unto you always.

Amen

The Way of Mastery Outline

Pathway of Enlightenment

The book you hold in your hands is part of a larger body of work, namely *The Way of Mastery*.

The Way of Mastery is a pathway offering a profound and comprehensive theology and lived experience of love via a progression of teachings, exercises, and *Living Practices*, all devoted to a genuine – and radical – depth of living enlightenment.

This depth goes beyond intellectual belief or the acceptance of certain concepts and ideas. It guides the student into their essential and eternal Heart, into a radical, transfigured gnosis, a 'knowledge by being that which is known.'

The purpose of *The Way of Mastery Pathway* is threefold:

~ To create a pathway that can support any student from their first steps all the way to truly awakening into 'Christ Mind'

~ To restore the original Teachings of Jeshua (Jesus) given to His followers

~ To 'birth a million Christs'

The Way of Mastery Pathway is comprised of four essential and interconnected parts:

~ The Jeshua Channelings: *The Jeshua Letters, The*

238

Early Years, The Way of the Servant, The Christ Mind Trilogy: The Way of the Heart, The Way of Transformation and The Way of Knowing and The Later Years.

~ **The Living Practices**: a series of alchemical trainings and Aramaic teachings, including *LovesBreath, In the Name* meditation, *The Aramaic Lord's Prayer, The Aramaic Beatitudes, Radical Inquiry,* the seamless life and more.

~ **Facilitated Teachings and Sacred Journeys:** deepening into a spiritual path often requires support; private sessions, workshops, seminars, on-line classes, sacred pilgrimages and a host of classes and gatherings are led by *Pathway* teachers.

~ **Temple Canyon Sanctuary:** sacred land near Abiquiu, New Mexico, miraculously purchased in the early days of the Pathway, and meant for future steps of development, as given specifically by Jeshua during the time of its purchase.

∞

In summary, *The Way of Mastery* is a Pathway of Enlightenment that re-establishes Jeshua's original teachings, and in doing so, it offers a profound, in-depth roadmap to support any soul from the first inkling to awaken all the way into knowing their most essential Self.

The *Pathway* aims at nothing less than a radical shift of identity from 'Ego' to 'Christ,' aiding students to increasingly live in and create from Christ Mind, itself.

Through His *Pathway* Jeshua seeks nothing less than the birthing of "a million Christs" on this planet and the transformation of the experience of humanity from fear to Love—the manifestation of Heaven on Earth that 'completes the very need for Time.'

Jayem is the channel of *The Way of Mastery*.

The Way of Mastery Pathway and its contents are copyright (c) Jayem.

Official Website: www.wayofmastery.com

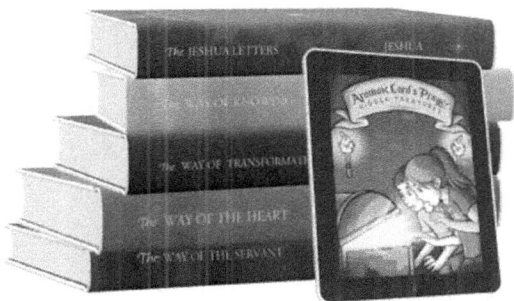

WAY OF MASTERY PATHWAY

The *Way of Mastery Pathway* offers a comprehensive road map if you have the desire to **grow,** to **heal** and to **know yourself.**

Find out more about what is available by visiting our website:
www.wayofmastery.com

WAY *of* MASTERY
www.wayofmastery.com

www.ingramcontent.com/pod-product-compliance
Lightning Source LLC
Chambersburg PA
CBHW031946090426
42739CB00006B/100